HORSE

♥ FUN

First published in the United States of America in 2019 by
Trafalgar Square Books
North Pomfret, Vermont 05053

Originally published in the German language as *Pferde und Reiten* by Franckh-Kosmos Verlags-GmbH & Co. KG, Stuttgart, Germany, 2016

Disclaimer of Liability
The author and publisher shall have neither liability nor responsibility to any person or entity with respect to any loss or damage caused or alleged to be caused directly or indirectly by the information contained in this book. While the book is as accurate as the author can make it, there may be errors, omissions, and inaccuracies.

Trafalgar Square Books encourages the use of approved riding helmets in all equestrian sports and activities.

ISBN: 9781570769085
Library of Congress Control Number: 2018961113

All photographs by Horst Streitferdt/KOSMOS, except: pp. 22, 26, 43, 74, 75, 76 top, middle, 77, 84, 85 bottom (Pauline von Hardenberg/KOSMOS); pp. 58 right bottom (Christiane Slawik/KOSMOS); pp. 52 bottom, 61 bottom, 63 a, 65 bottom left, right, 67 top, middle, 74 bottom, 86 bottom (Gudrun Braun); p. 8 (Geza Farkas-fotolia.com and Eric Isselée-fotolia.com (Stockmaßabbildung); pp.14, 15 bag (magnia-fotolia.com); pp. 58 (Klaus Eppele-fotolia.com); p. 59 hay (Africa Studio-fotolia.com), carrots (rduzl-fotolia.com), dandelions (emer-fotolia.com), apples (Dionisvera-fotolia.com); p. 63 c (Petra Echerl-fotolia.com); p. 71 (nemlep-fotolia.com, Victoria Makarova-fotolia.com); pp. 4, 16, 46, 56, 78, 90 (quilli-fotolia.com, aopsan-fotolia.com, Ragnarocks-fotolia.com, by-studio-fotolia.com, picsfive-fotolia.com).

All illustrations by Anike Hage, except: pp. 9,13 grooming, 19, 22 saddles, 35 rider, wooden horse, 42, 43 arena diagrams, 44 bottom middle, 61 top middle (Esther von Hacht).

Cover design by RM Didier and Christine Sassie using Illustrations by Anike Hage, Esther von Hacht (grooming tools) and a photo by Horst Streitferdt/KOSMOS.

Interior design by Christine Sassie

Printed in China

10 9 8 7 6 5 4 3 2 1

OPEN if You're WILD About Horses!

Facts and activities for horse-crazy kids

HORSE FUN

For Real Horse Lovers ONLY

By

Gudrun Braun,

Anne Scheller,

and Anike Hage

Translated by

Emma Josephine Didier

T

Trafalgar Square

North Pomfret, Vermont

Hi There, I'm Maxi!

My biggest dream ever came true. Wait, no – not my biggest dream, because that's to own my own horse. But right after that comes my second biggest dream: learning how to ride. Hobbit is the pony I get to ride at the barn where I take lessons. I am so happy when I'm with him. Whether I'm grooming him, walking him, grazing him, or riding him, he's just my favorite and I love him. If I could, I'd buy him! But first I have to prove to my parents and Susan, my riding teacher, that I'm a good rider and want to learn to be a good horse person.

Do you want to know what I'm learning about and experiencing at the barn where I take riding lessons? In my journal, you can read all about everything I've found out about horses since I started riding. When I'm not riding, I like to do arts and crafts. I've made some pretty cool horsey things all by myself out of paper and fabric. Join me! And if you want to know what type of horse and riding style suit you, there are some quizzes that will help you find out.

Off we go!

This is Hobbit, the pony I get to ride in lessons! He is super good and patient – just the perfect horse for beginners.

My whole name is Maximiliane – my parents thought I would be a boy!

Riding Is My Sport!

Let's go, Hobbit!

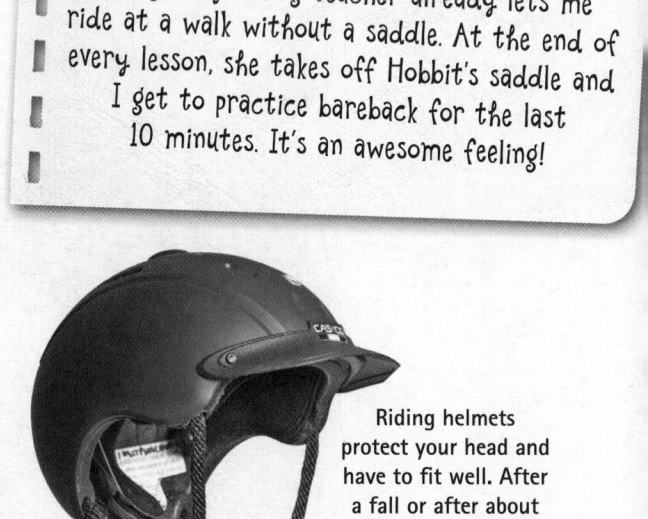

What I like best of all is to take Hobbit out for a ride, for hours, through the woods and meadows. But there are so many other ways to have fun with horses: jumping, dressage, Western riding, vaulting, driving, trick training, groundwork.

What Do You Need to Ride?

Find a riding stable that offers lessons for beginners. You can find barns in your area by searching online or through word of mouth. Otherwise you can start at a horse camp – that can be great, too – riding, grooming, tacking up, and hanging with horses and other kids every day. To start, you'll need an approved helmet, boots with a small heel (so your feet don't slip through the stirrups), and comfortable pants without a seam on the inside of the legs.

My dream: Soon, I'll be galloping bareback through the fields! So far I haven't dared, though. My riding teacher already lets me ride at a walk without a saddle. At the end of every lesson, she takes off Hobbit's saddle and I get to practice bareback for the last 10 minutes. It's an awesome feeling!

Riding Helmet

Dressage whips are about 4 feet (1.2 meters) long. They are used for riding and groundwork.

Gloves

Breeches

Crop

Chaps

Riding Boots

Riding helmets protect your head and have to fit well. After a fall or after about two years of wearing it, you should buy a new one.

Riding boots are often combined with chaps or worn with jodhpurs. Chaps are worn over your pants and made of soft leather.

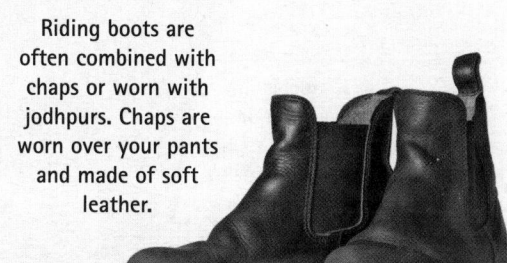

HORSE SPORTS

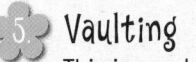

1. Dressage
Enhances the horse's natural gaits and movement through gymnastic exercises. Part of the basic training for every horse and rider.

2. Eventing
Composed of three phases: dressage, cross-country riding, and show jumping.

3. Western Riding
There are lots of options if you prefer riding in a Western saddle: reining, cutting, roping, pleasure, Western or Cowboy Dressage, working ranch, and more!

4. Show Jumping
You've probably seeing show jumping on TV. The point is not to knock down any rails and to be the fastest through the course. At the most difficult level there are at least 10 obstacles that can be well over 5 feet (1.5 meters) high!

5. Vaulting
This is acrobatic gymnastics on horseback, while the horse canters on a longe line. You can compete indi-vidually or in a group.

6. Baroque Riding
Breeds like Andalusians, Lusitanos, Friesians, and Lipizzaners are used by riders who enjoy performing classical dressage (sometimes in a fine velvet coat!).

7. Driving
This sport can be done with one, two, or four horses pulling a cart or carriage. There are show ring competitions and races around obstacles.

Maxi's Tip

To convince my parents that I take riding seriously, I saved up my allowance and bought my own riding helmet. For my birthday, though, maybe they will get me my own riding boots and chaps!

3

THE FIRST RIDING LESSON

Excited, in love, and totally happy!

Finally! Today was the day: I had my first riding lesson! The barn I went to was really close to our house. It was so awesome! But I guess I'd better start from the beginning. Man, I was so excited! Tom, my older brother, was super annoyed because I kept jumping up and down in front of the TV. Robin and Phil just rolled their eyes and then went to go play soccer. It was just Leo who was happy for me. But he's also just two years old and is almost always laughing. Four brothers, two parents, but zero horse fans in my family! Can you imagine?!

Mom and I rode our bikes to the barn. Right away my mom went up to the first girl we saw and started asking her a bunch of questions. I felt a bit embarrassed. The girl's name was Elena and she pointed us to Susan, the riding teacher. She has her own horse, a huge Friesian with a long mane. She's strict and kind of cool, but also nice. Mom said goodbye and Susan brought me over to one of the stalls. Inside was Hobbit. I saw him and fell in love right away. He has such a beautiful red-brown coat, a long mane, and HUGE loyal eyes. Hobbit is so cute!

Then I was a bit suprised because Susan just walked away. She said I should make friends with Hobbit. "Just be nice and calm and speak in a low voice," she said. And there I stood. "Hello, Hobbit," I whispered. He looked at me and wiggled his ears back and forth. Then he stuck out his nose. I raised my hand to pet him, and he took a step back. "Don't be scared, it's just me, Maxi," I explained to him. "I'm so excited to start riding. I'll always be nice to you, Hobbit." He came a bit closer again and then I was allowed to pet him. His coat was so soft...it was heavenly!

A little bit later, Susan called all the beginners into the barn aisle. Aside from me there were two other girls and one boy: Lissy, Tanya, and Jacob. Susan showed us the grooming tools and then we got to groom Paul, a really sweet Haflinger. I kept looking over to catch a glimpse of Hobbit, who had his head sticking out of his stall window. He's so cute!

When it was time to go back over to him, Elena came along and helped me with the grooming, haltering, and saddling. I would have never been able to do it on my own – it's super difficult! Elena is 15 and started riding forever ago. She taught me a lot. Finally I was allowed to mount – or so I thought. First came another thing: I was supposed to lead Hobbit! To do that I had to walk alongside him on his left side. I held the reins in my hand. We crossed the barn aisle and went into the indoor arena, following the others.

Susan attached a long rope called a longe line to Hobbit's bridle. Elena kept an eye on Lissy, Tanya, and Jacob. Susan showed me how to put my foot in the stirrup, and all of a sudden I was sitting up there! It was a phenomenal feeling. Hobbit always moved around a little bit, even when he was standing in one spot, and I could feel him really well. Then he started walking in a circle around Susan on the longe line. Riding feels amazing! There's a sway to it and it's very comfy. I can't wait until I can finally go to my second riding lesson! I'm excited for all the things I'll have to talk about afterward.

Hobbit

Your Secret Pony Diary

Learning to ride is so exciting and ponies are just too cute! Luckily I can write about all of it in my journal: the riding lessons, the other riding students, and of course Hobbit. I also like to glue photos of Hobbit in my journal, write down the birthdays of my friends from the barn or important horse knowledge, and much, much more... Let me show you how you can make your very own diary!

What you need:

- White and color cardboard (1 piece each)
- Pencil and scissors
- Colorful tape and glue
- Different color cardboard (2 pieces)
- A scrap of thick cardboard
- Markers and stickers and any other decorations you may like
- White paper (about 20 pages)
- Hole-punch
- 4 book-bindng rings (available at arts-and-crafts stores)

I wish I could spend all my days and nights at the barn! But since my parents won't allow that, I've got my journal. It's super fun to flip through the pages and read about all of the things I've experienced together with Hobbit!

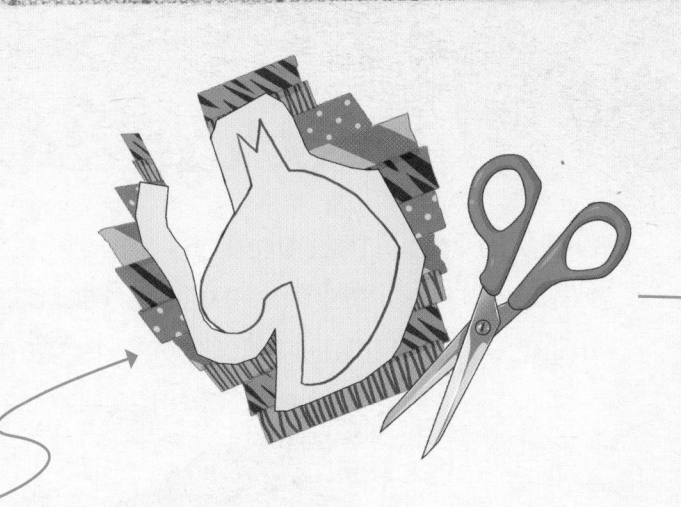

1. Horse's Head

Draw the outline of a horse's head on the white cardboard. Don't worry if you mess up – you won't be able to see it later. Roughly cut out the outline, leaving space around the lines you drew, and cover the reverse side of the cutout with color tape. Next neatly cut along the outline of the horse's head. Lastly, glue the horse's head onto the colorful cardboard and cut out around it so the color frames it.

2. Diary Cover

Glue the horse head onto one of the other color cardboard pieces. If you glue a couple of strips of cotton in the spot first, before you glue the horse head down, it will look like it's floating – pretty neat! Now you can decorate the cover of your journal any way you want.

3. Book and Pen

Place the blank white paper between the front and back covers. Punch four holes down the left side and insert the book-binding rings to hold everything together. You can even hook your pen onto one of the rings! Add pages if needed later on.

> Some things I put in my journal are pictures of Hobbit, barn friends' birthdays, and riding tips I've learned...how about you?

Maxi's Tip

Instead of a horse's head, you could also draw a horseshoe, a heart, or something else. You can also glue two ribbons to the middle inside of the front and back covers and tie a bow to close up your journal.

The Horse Family

Did you know that donkeys and zebras are also part of the horse family? Ponies are horses that are shorter than 14.2 hands tall (a "hand" is 4 inches). You should also know the names of different coat colors and markings so you can describe your horse.

Shire Horse: 17 hands

14 hands

Connemara Pony: 14 hands

Shetland Pony: 7 hands

How Tall?

The height of a horse is measured at the withers. The withers is the highest point along the transition between the horse's neck and back. It is the location of the upward-pointing spinous process of one of the horse's vertebrae.

Archaeological records from Mongolia show that humans started domesticating wild horses 6,000 years ago.

Donkeys are part of the horse family. Wild donkeys live in the dry regions of Africa and Asia. Typical donkey traits include long ears, an upright mane, a tassel on the tail, and very hard hooves.

My Striped Horse?

Can you ride zebras? In fact, you can't; it doesn't work at all. Even though baby zebras are sometimes raised by humans in Africa, you can't tame them. When they grow up they won't want anything to do with people anymore. I think their stripes are absolutely beautiful. Every zebra has its own pattern of stripes, just like your fingerprint is totally unique in the world.

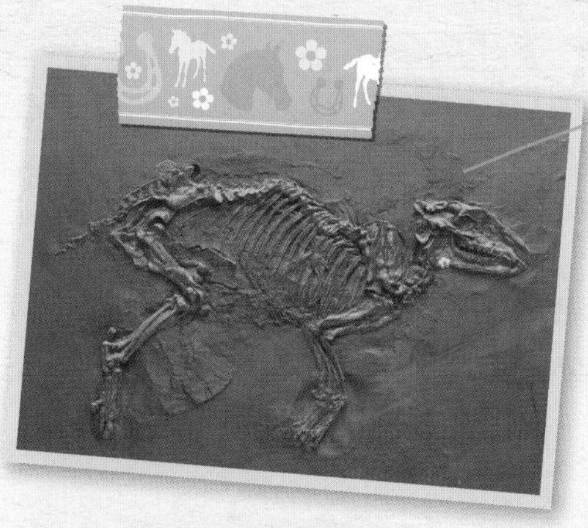

The fossil of an approximately 50-million-year-old Eohippus, which was about as big as a fox.

40 million years later ...

Nice to meet you! My name is Pliohippus. I lived about 10 million years ago.

... another 10 million years later ...

The Ancestors

Today's horses descended from the Eohippus, which lived about 50 million years ago and was only about as big as a fox. It hid under bushes and ate leaves and fruits. From the Eohippus evolved the Pliohippus, which ate mostly grasses and looked a lot more like a horse.

Coat Colors and Markings

Think about your favorite-colored horse. Bay, chestnut, gray, black, and pinto are the terms for horses with the most common coat colors. Icelandic Horses are particularly diverse in color – they come in over 100 different colors. Spots on a horse's head or legs of a different color from the rest of the coat are called "markings." You've probably heard the term "blaze" before. For leg markings, the part of the leg determines the name: sock, coronet, or stocking, for example.

BLAZE

SNIP

BALD FACE

4. 5. 6.

FAINT STAR

STAR

STAR AND STRIPE

1. 2. 3.

HORSE SMARTS

Coat Colors

1. I am a brown horse.

2. My coat is called Palomino.

3. + 4. We are chestnut.

5. My coat is called liver chestnut.

6. I am a bay.

Mom, Dad, Kid

Horses don't live in small families, but rather in larger groups that have a certain hierarchy to them. Several other horses at the barn where I ride are a part of Hobbit's herd, and they've all known each other for a long time and get along splendidly.

A Horse's Life Stages

Horses are born after a gestation period of 11 months. When they are about one year old, their mothers stop nursing them. At about four years old they are fully grown. They are sexually mature at two years old. Ponies can live to be up to 40 years old, but horses usually don't live longer than 30 years. You can tell a horse's approximate age from the degree of wear on his teeth. The teeth are worn down and deformed over time from chewing roughage. Sometimes, an old horse's teeth can be so worn down that he can only eat soft meals.

In wild herds of horses, stallions, mares, and foals live together with other horse families. In most barns, however, stallions are kept separately from other horses.

Hey cutie! Won't you come over to me?

Foaling Season

A newborn foal gets up on his legs shortly after he's born and has to begin walking to keep up with the rest of the herd. In wild herds, foals are nursed by their mothers until they have another foal, so for about one year. Foals are very playful and curious. If you are near one and talk to him, he'll come right up to you. Watch out for his mother, though, as mares are always looking to protect their foals.

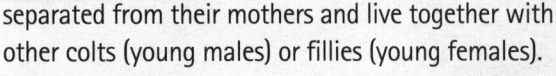

HORSE ENCYCLOPEDIA

Mare

Female horse. The external genitalia are located at the dock of the tail. The udder can be seen between the hind legs, but only when the mare is nursing a foal.

Colt or Filly

Young horses up to three years old. They nurse until they are about six months old; then they are usually separated from their mothers and live together with other colts (young males) or fillies (young females).

Gelding

A castrated male horse, which is well-suited for riding. Geldings are can no longer reproduce because their testes are removed in an operation that usually takes place before they reach sexual maturity.

Stallion

Male horse. Defining characteristics include the sheath, which surrounds and protects the penis, and two testes between the hind legs. Stallions are generally stronger and more tempestuous than geldings or mares.

Estrus

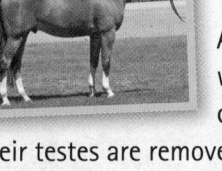

The period of time when mares are receptive to mating ("in heat"): March through September, six to eight days every three or four weeks, so that foals are born when it's warm and there is enough food.

Pregnancy

A horse's gestation period lasts about 11 months. It's not until the end of these 11 months that you begin to notice a change in behavior and the big belly that signify that a mare will soon give birth.

Birth

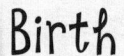

Foals are born forelegs and head first. After giving birth lying down, the mare stands up, severing the umbilical cord and causing the amniotic sac to rip. The foal then begins breathing.

Nursing

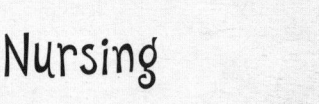

During the first two months of their life, foals drink exclusively their mother's milk. The first milk they drink is crucial; it contains antibodies that strengthen the immune system.

Hierarchy

Horses are much safer when they live together in large groups where a leader decides where to go. The social hierarchy of a herd often changes, as new horses join the herd.

Herd

Horses live together in herds. As a group they are better protected from predators. Horses communicate with one another through body language.

My Beautiful Horse

I love grooming Hobbit. It's so nice to brush his soft coat and listen to his contented snorts. I feel very proud when his coat shines. It's just picking his hooves that's a bit scary. You know?

Grooming

You should groom your horse either in the stable aisle or in another designated grooming site. It's not a great idea to groom your horse in his stall. Secure your horse in a safe, quiet, calm way with cross-ties or another quick-release tie and his halter. Make sure to leave plenty of space between your horse and others. Consider whether your horse gets along well with nearby horses.

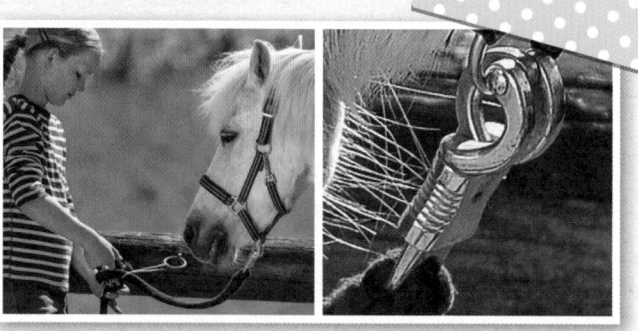

Safe Tie Option   Panic Snap

Safety Knot

Since horses are flight animals, being tied up goes against their natural instinct. Horses thus have to gain trust in humans and learn over time that being tied up doesn't present any danger to them. Fasten your horse using a rope with a panic snap and safety knot so it can come undone quickly. When a horse pulls back on a rope without a release, there's a high risk of a head or spine injury.

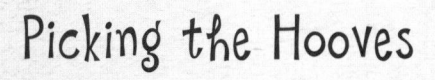

Picking the Hooves

Caring for a horse's hooves is only possible if the horse coope-rates. Hobbit learned to lift his leg when he hears a certain command. I stand right next to his leg, bend over, and say, "Give." While I'm holding the hoof with one hand, I scratch and brush the grooves on either side of the "frog" carefully until they are clean. Susan says, "Remain focused and patient in case your horse won't pick up his foot, pulls away, or wriggles around. Ask someone to help if you need it."

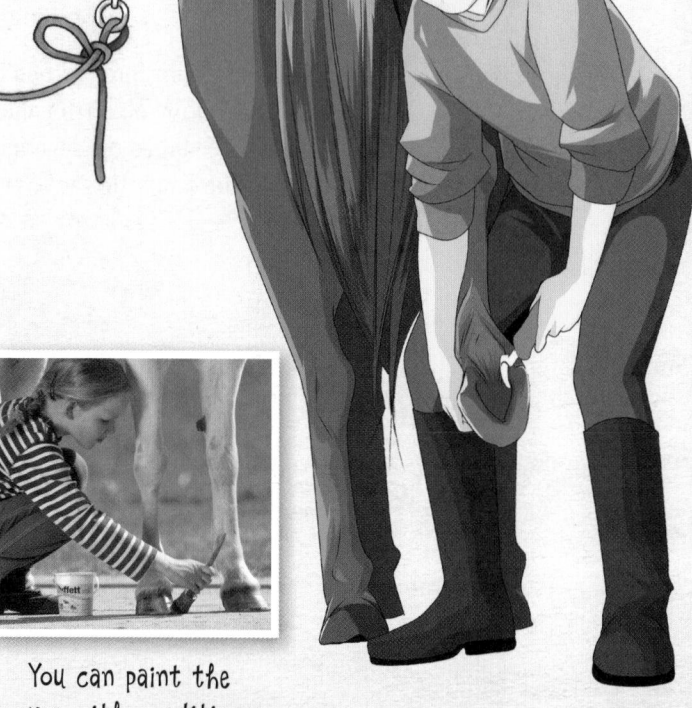

You can paint the hooves with conditioner.

MY GROOMING PLAN

1. Carefully brush the head with a soft brush and tidy up the mane and forelock with a comb.

2. Roughly brush off any dirt on the body and rump using the curry comb. On the legs, use a coarse grooming brush. Skip over any sensitive or un-muscled body parts.

3. Use a soft grooming brush to brush off remaining dust and smooth out the coat, occasionally rubbing the brush against the curry comb to clean it. Hit the curry comb against your boot every now and then to knock the dirt out of it. Lastly, use a soft towel to polish the coat until it shines.

4. Untangle the tail.

5. Use the coarse grooming brush to clean the outside of the hooves and a hoof pick for the inside.

6. If necessary, clean the eyes, nostrils, and mouth (one sponge) and penis or udder and anus (a different sponge) carefully with lukewarm water, always making sure to rinse out the sponge thoroughly.

Curry comb and soft grooming brush.

Coarse grooming brush.

Check out page 87 to learn how to braid or band the mane.

GROOMING GEAR

Curry Comb

Sponge

Soft Brush

Sweat Scraper

Hoof Pick

Mane Comb

Coarse Brush

Towel

Untangling the tail.

Tail Tip

"Hold on, don't brush the tail!" Susan exclaims. "Sorry, but we would lose too many tail hairs. We want Hobbit to look his best. Remove any hay or shavings. Carefully pull apart individual strands. If the tail is super dirty, we'll wash it."

Colorful Grooming Tote Bag

With my allowance I can afford to buy myself a hoof pick or a curry comb, but nice grooming boxes are really expensive! I decided to create my own super cool grooming gear bag. It's really easy – do you want to see how it's done?

For the stamps you will need:

- Pieces of foam rubber and a pen
- Scissors and craft glue
- Small wooden blocks
- Kitchen knife and apples
- 8 corks and some string

♥ 1. A Very Horsey Bag

Paint the rubber stamps with some fabric paint – but not too thick. Stamp lots of hearts and a horse head onto your bag and let them dry. Use a paintbrush to add details, like eyes, mouth, and nostrils, and writing.

♥ 1. Foam Rubber Stamps

Sketch a few shapes onto the pieces of foam rubber and cut them out. Try not to make them too small or detailed. How about a horse head, a heart, a star, or a horse shoe? Glue each piece of rubber onto a wooden block.

2. Apple Stamps

Cut the apple in half.

3. Cork Flowers

Arrange seven corks so that one is in the center and the others surround it. Use a little bit of glue to stick them all together and then tie a string around them tightly. Together they make a large flower; a single cork can create a small flower.

Put a piece of cardboard into the bag so that the paint doesn't leak through onto the other side. Try your stamp out on a piece of scrap fabric, first.

Maxi + Hobbit

Best friends forever

② Cute Apple Bag

Apply a thin layer of paint onto one of the apple halves and press it against your bag to print an apple shape onto it. Use the other half for a different color.
Looks good enough to eat, right?

③ Flower Bag

Paint some grass onto the bottom half of your bag with a paintbrush and let it dry. Apply a thin layer of paint onto your big cork flower – one color for the outside ring of corks and a different color for the center cork. Stamp some flowers onto your bag. With a single cork you can print some small flowers directly into the grass.

For your tote bags you will need:

- Fabric paint
- Cloth bag and fabric scraps
- Piece of cardboard
- Homemade stamps

Maxi's Tip

I have a curry comb and grooming brushes made of light-colored wood. I sanded the wood down a bit using some sandpaper and painted them with acrylic paint to match my grooming tote bag.

Stable Air and Horse Scent

I'll do anything for Hobbit – even sweeping and mucking!

It's another whole week until my next riding lesson. Basically an eternity! I dreamed of Hobbit three nights in a row. I dreamed that we rode over fields, crossed a creek, galloped beneath the trees, and made a campfire. It really was amazing! I spent three days down on my knees begging Mom and Dad to pay for more riding lessons (the outcome: "No"). I raved on and on about Hobbit to my best friends Cleo and Rana (the outcome: they plug their ears as soon as I utter the word "pony"). Tom, Robin, Phil, and Leo never listen to me anyway. On the fourth day, something had to happen.

I rode my bike to the barn. It was really bustling there: horses were being groomed and saddled, kids were being dropped off by car, somewhere in the distance, a horse neighed.

Hobbit wasn't in his stall, but I found him in the arena. A young boy was riding him, and for some reason, I thought it was really dumb that he got to ride Hobbit. He's my favorite! "Hey, Maxi!" someone yelled in a loud voice. It was Susan. I wasn't sure if she was going to yell at me...are you even allowed to just "show up" at the barn when you don't have a lesson? But she was really nice. "Did you miss Hobbit?" she asked.

I nodded. "And I missed the smell here in the barn and the neighing and the grooming stuff and, well, everything. One week is suuuuch a long time!"

Susan grinned. I think she understood. "Listen, Maxi, I have an idea," she said. "You can come here in the afternoons whenever you want and help out with some of the barn chores, like mucking, feeding, sweeping, and grooming – stuff like that. In return you get to ride a little extra every now and then. Of course, only after a few months when you've become more secure on horseback. Would you like that?"

I grinned from ear to ear. "Yes, yes, yessss!" I cheered.

"I'm warning you, it's hard work." Susan added. "Elena!" she called out. "Maxi's going to help you out, okay?"

Elena nodded. "Hey, Maxi!" she said. "Why don't you come with me right away? I was

just about to start cleaning saddles."

We got two saddles and put them on saddle stands. "Soap and conditioner for the saddles are in the closet in the tack room," said Elena. "The door on the left. Bring a few rags, too, they're at the very top."

"Okay." I already knew where the tack room was, but there weren't any closets in there with doors!

"How much longer are you going to take?" Elena yelled impatiently from outside.

"I'm coming!" Thank goodness at that moment Lissy, from my riding group, came in. "Do you know where the closet is?" I asked desperately.

She didn't say anything but opened a door. An actual door! I thought it led to the barn, but nooo, behind it there was a closet full of grooming and cleaning gear, including soap, conditioner, and rags for tack. Oops! Luckily, Lissy just grinned and didn't say anything about it to Elena.

We cleaned and conditioned the saddles, which smelled really good. After that we mucked out the stalls, which did not smell as good! Plus it was hard work! You gotta dig your pitchfork straight into the piles, lift up and fill the wheelbarrow, and off it goes to the manure heap. I thought about Hobbit the entire time, which helped make the mucking a little bit fun. After all, I want Hobbit to have a nice, clean stall. You can't ride horses without mucking, that much is for sure. After we cleaned stalls, Susan asked me to sweep the stable aisle, and after that, I was totally drained.

"Alright, let's call it a day," Susan said. "It's closing time now for everyone, even the horses. Do you want to bring Hobbit out to the paddock?"

You bet I wanted to! Hobbit was in the aisle, tied up with a lead rope. Susan led two horses out: Cicero and Caesar. Elena had two others, whose names I didn't know yet. Hobbit just walked along behind me – I didn't even have to do anything. All the better; that way I could relax and enjoy the moment. Just me, Hobbit, and a nose full of pony aroma.

Parts of the Horse

Cannon, withers, dock...some of the parts of a horse have some really strange names. I really enjoy learning them all though, because I'm dying to pass the test Susan gives new riders. For the test you have to be able to name all the parts, right there on a live horse. Why don't you join me studying?

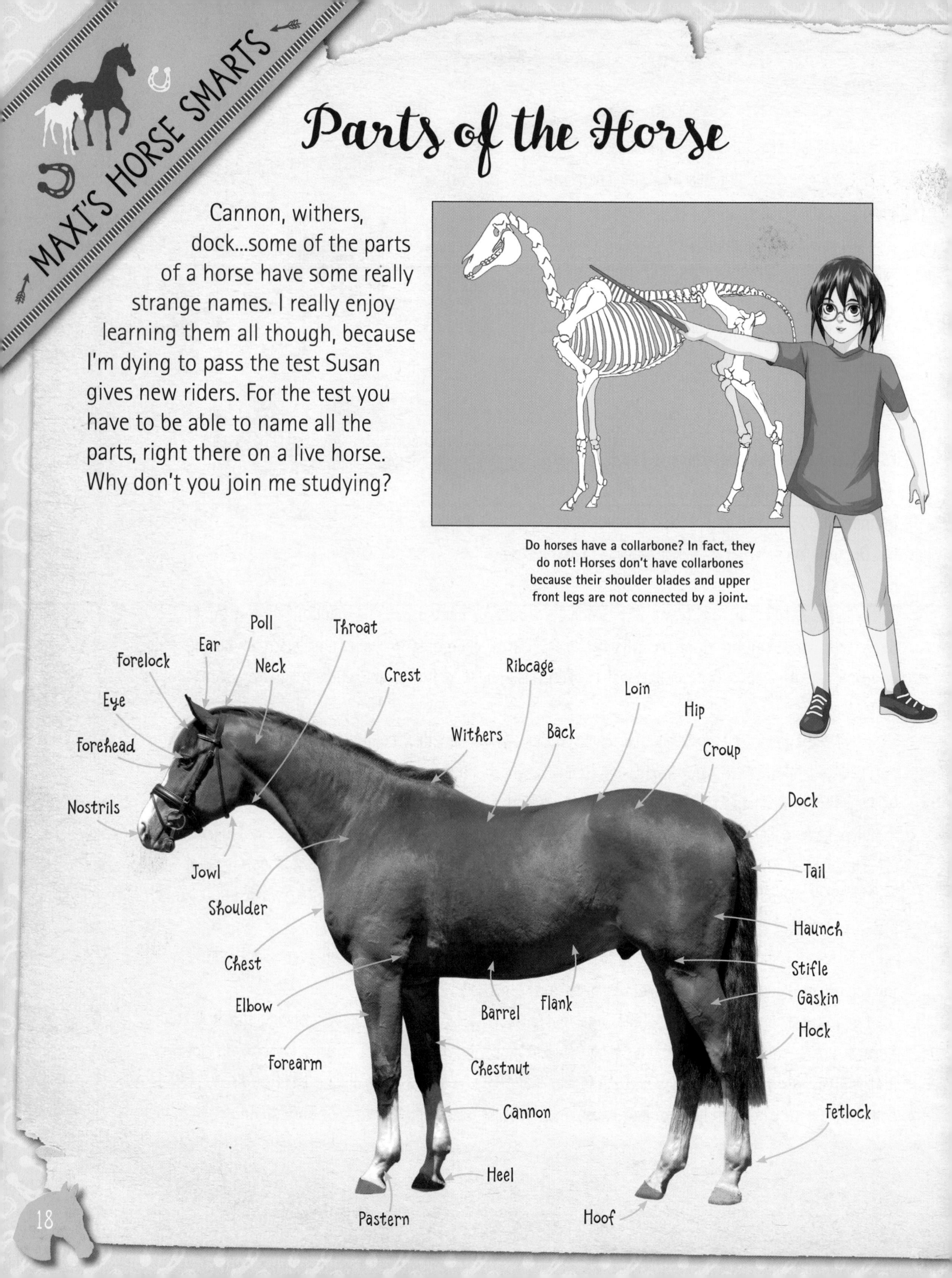

Do horses have a collarbone? In fact, they do not! Horses don't have collarbones because their shoulder blades and upper front legs are not connected by a joint.

Poll
Ear
Throat
Forelock
Neck
Ribcage
Loin
Eye
Crest
Hip
Forehead
Withers
Back
Croup
Nostrils
Dock
Jowl
Tail
Shoulder
Haunch
Chest
Stifle
Elbow
Flank
Gaskin
Barrel
Hock
Forearm
Chestnut
Cannon
Fetlock
Heel
Pastern
Hoof

Spines, Bones, and Joints

The skeleton of a horse is made up of nearly 210 bones. The majority of the spine is only slightly flexible since it has to carry the weight of the heavy digestive system. The neck and tail, on the other hand, are very mobile. The bones of the locomotive system are connected by joints and ligaments. Horses are unguligrades, meaning they walk on their toes – specifically the middle digit of their hands and feet.

Flexible neck and legs.

Esophagus

Stomach

Small Intestine

Rectum

Large Intestine

Muscles, Tendons, and Ligaments

Horses move in such a way as to save their strength, and generally they move slowly. They spend up to 20 hours a day grazing. However, when necessary they can break into a sprint. Over 700 muscles are responsible for their movements. The muscles are connected to bones with tendons and ligaments. The strongest one is the nuchal ligament, which supports the horse's heavy head.

Caution: Horse droppings.

Digestive System

The main food source for horses – grasses and roughage – do not contain many nutrients. For that reason, horses have to eat many small portions throughout the day. Their stomachs are relatively small, but the intestine is over 65 feet long. With help from gut bacteria, the nutrients are extracted from the food in the intestine.

Heart and Lungs

A horse's heart weighs about 8.8 lbs and pumps roughly 12 gallons of blood through the body. Nutrients and oxygen are transported to the organs via the bloodstream. A horse's lungs are almost three times as large as a human's. Horses can only breathe through their nostrils and can get sick from constantly breathing dusty or musty stable air. That's why it is important to be sure to take your horse out to the paddock or pasture, even in wintertime.

Taking the pulse.

Temperature, Pulse, Respiration = TPR

Horses have a resting pulse ranging from 28 to 40 beats per minute. The best spot to feel the pulse is on the underside of the head, between the jowls. Horses breathe between 8 and 16 times a minute, but that number can get up to 100 breaths per minute at a full gallop. You can see a horse's breathing by observing the ribcage or nostrils. The normal body temperature of an adult horse lies between 99.5° and 100.8° F. With high degrees of exertion, that temperature may rise up to 104° F. The horse's temperature is taken in the rectum.

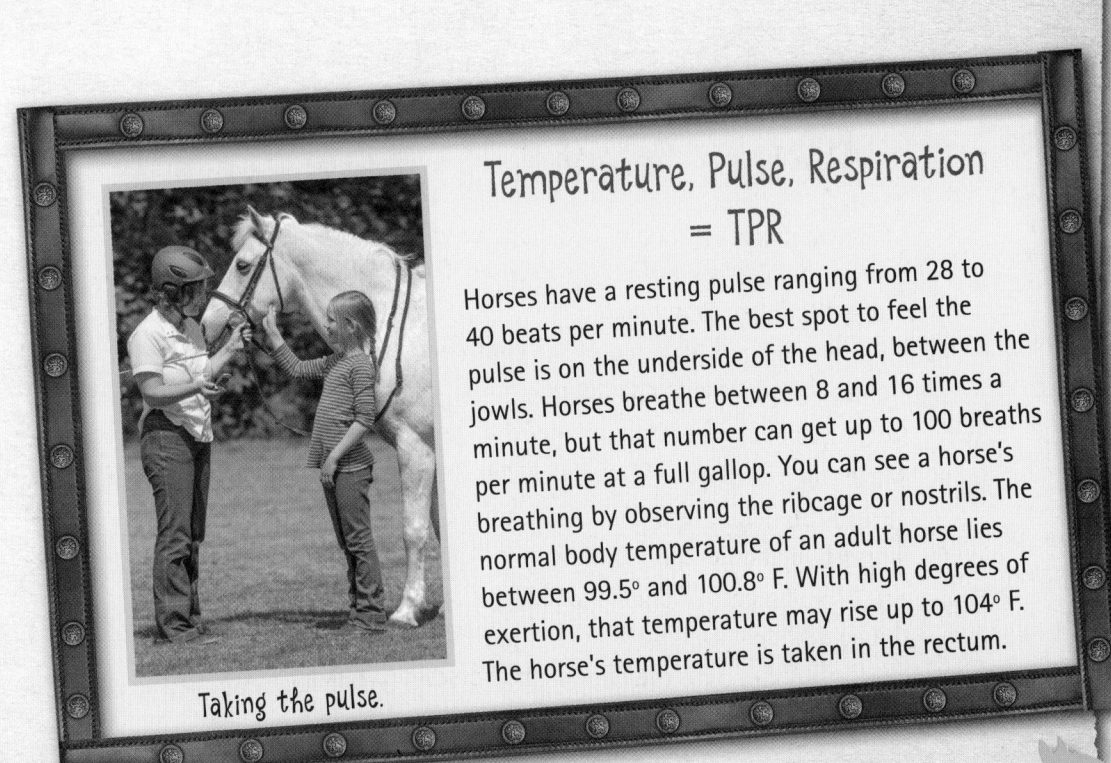

Picture Frames and "Luck Catchers"

You already knew that horseshoes are lucky charms, right? Next time the horses at your stable are shod, ask the farrier for some old shoes. That way you can bring that pony luck right into your own room!

Say cheese, Hobbit!

For the picture frame you'll need:

· A photograph and stiff cardboard
· Horseshoe
· Scissors and a pencil
· Double-sided tape
· About 20 inches of ribbon

1. Picture Frame

· Stick two pieces of double-sided tape onto the cardboard, remove the plastic cover on the exposed side of the tape, and stick the photo in place.
· Place the horseshoe on top of the photo and lightly trace around the edges with the pencil.
· Cut this shape out slightly smaller than you drew it.
· Make sure the photo fits nicely behind the horseshoe.
· Thread the ribbon through the two upper holes in the horseshoe and tie it in the back.
· Stick small pieces of double-sided tape onto the back of the horseshoe.
· Tape the photo onto the back of the horseshoe, making sure to tuck and hide the backs of the ribbon, too.

For the Luck Catcher you'll need:

- Horseshoe
- Yarn
- 8-10 beads
- Scissors
- Tape

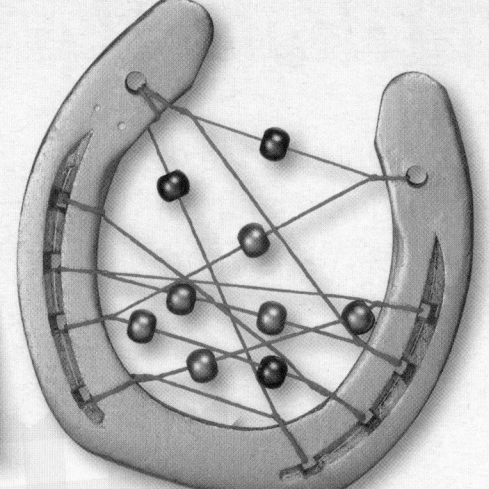

You can even make the beads yourself! For that, you need a triangle of paper approximately ¾ inch wide and 4 inches long. Roll the triangle starting at the base and tape down the tip.

2. Luck Catcher

- Cut a piece of yarn about 6½ feet long and thread one end through a hole in the horseshoe.
- Tie a knot in the back and tape it down.
- Thread the yarn back and forth through the holes of the horseshoe, adding beads as you go. A spider-web pattern should form.
- If you like the way your Luck Catcher turned out, tie another knot with the yarn at the back and tape it down.

Thread a piece of sturdy ribbon or thread through the top holes of the horseshoe to hang your Luck Catcher somewhere where you need a lot of good luck, like over your bed (to catch some sweet pony dreams) or over your desk (to help with your homework).

Where Does Good Luck Come From?

Back in the day, iron was very valuable. Finding a horseshoe was sort of like finding money on the street is for us nowadays.

By the way, always make sure to hang up your horseshoe with the opening facing up. Otherwise all the good luck will fall out!

Right

Wrong

Maxi's Tip

Before starting the horseshoe your project, scrub with a wire brush. If you want, paint it your favorite color!

Tacking Up

It's pretty complicated to get the bit into the horse's mouth and then pull the headpiece over the ears. Susan checks to see if my bridle and saddle are on properly before every lesson.

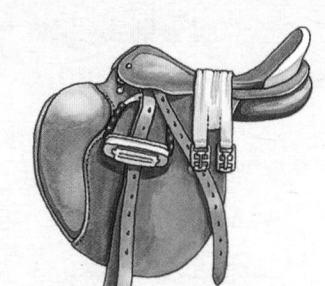

Jumping Saddle

Saddling

- Carry the saddle with both hands, with the girth resting on top.
- Lift it up above the horse's back from the left side of the horse (called the "near side") and place it with the front at the withers.
- Slide it backward into the fitting position. That way you make sure the hair beneath is smooth and flat.
- There should be no folds in the saddle pad. Be sure to check on the right-hand side (called the "off side") as well.
- Let the girth hang down, and walk around to the other side to secure it to the saddle.
- The girth is secured by two straps called billets. The third is there as a safety, in case one of the others breaks.

Checking stirrup length.

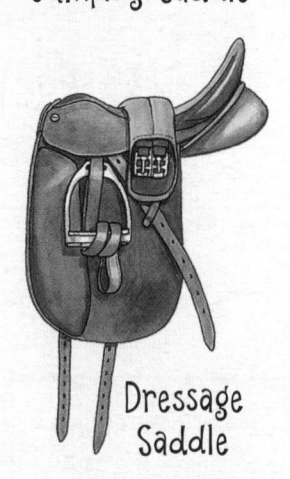

Dressage Saddle

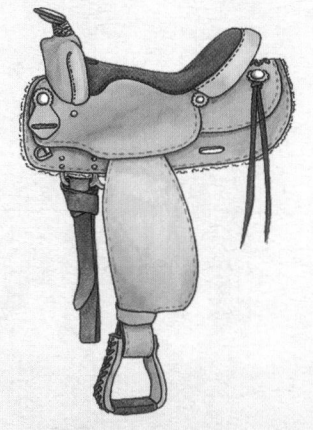

All-Purpose Saddle

Western Saddle

Bridling

Take the bridle, place the reins around the horse's neck, remove the halter, hold the bit in your left hand and the bridle in your right, and place the bit gently into the horse's mouth, pulling the headpiece over his eyes and ears. The buckles should be fastened from "top to bottom": the throatlatch (leave a fist's width of space), the noseband, and then the chinstrap if using a flash (leave two fingers of space in both cases). Pull the horse's forelock over the browband, tidy up the mane, take the reins back over the horse's neck, and hold them with both hands. All done!

1. Removing the halter.

2. Placing the bit in the mouth.

3. Fastening the throatlatch.

About Bridles

There are many different types of bridles, bits, and martingales. Most lesson barns should be equipped with plain bridles and snaffle bits. It's really important that the bridle and bit are neither too wide nor too narrow. Most horses are comfortable wearing a snaffle bit in the mouth. The snaffle is made of metal, has a link in the middle, and lies on the horse's tongue and across the jaw in the position where the horse naturally has no teeth ("bars"). The straps of the bridle keep the bit attached securely to the head. Note there should be two fingers of space under the nose and flash strap so that the horse can breathe comfortably.

DID YOU KNOW ...

... when removing a bridle, you should unfasten the buckles from "bottom to top": first the chinstrap (on a flash), then the noseband, and finally the throatlatch. Wait for the horse to "spit" the bit out on his own so that it doesn't hit against his teeth.

Maxi's Tip

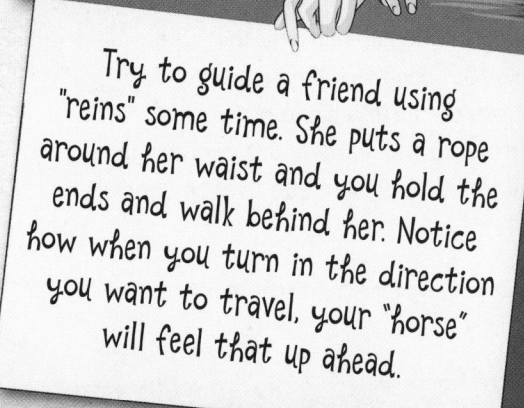

Try to guide a friend using "reins" some time. She puts a rope around her waist and you hold the ends and walk behind her. Notice how when you turn in the direction you want to travel, your "horse" will feel that up ahead.

Mounting...and Staying On!

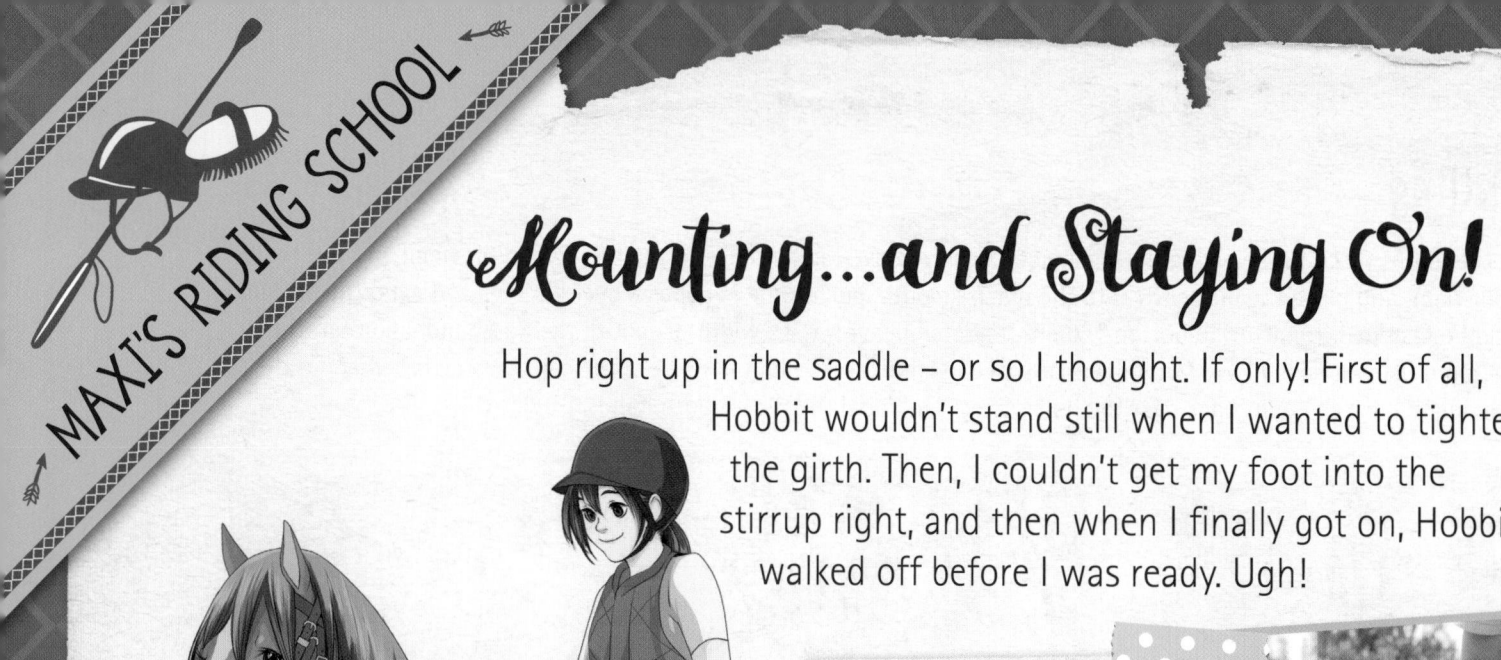

Hop right up in the saddle – or so I thought. If only! First of all, Hobbit wouldn't stand still when I wanted to tighten the girth. Then, I couldn't get my foot into the stirrup right, and then when I finally got on, Hobbit walked off before I was ready. Ugh!

Unless you're super-duper athletic or a gymnast, you should only get on a horse from a mounting block or with the help of a friend.

Mounting Correctly

- Tighten the girth on the left-hand side of the horse.
- Adjust the stirrups on both sides, checking the length against the length of your arm.
- To go easy on both the saddle and the horse, use a mounting block to get on.
- Put your left foot in the stirrup, hold the reins with your left hand, and hold on to the saddle.
- Pull yourself up, slide gently into the saddle, and slip your other foot into the right stirrup.
- Check the stirrup length one more time.

Dismounting

- Take both feet out of the stirrups. Only then can you start getting down.
- Swing your leg up and over the croup, but don't kick the horse!
- Loosen the girth a bit, run the stirrups up the leathers and secure them, and pull the reins up and over the horse's head.

Riding backward without a saddle only works because Hobbit is so well behaved and experienced! If you ever want to try it out, ask your riding teacher first.

Dressage Seat

Facing forward, straighten your back, keep your hips loose, slightly angle your elbows so that your arms are in line with the horse's mouth, and keep your hands loosely closed, holding the reins in your fists without clenching them. Let your legs hang loose with your thighs in contact with the horse, and place the stirrups just under the balls of your feet.

This is how it's done: your elbows, arms, hands, the reins, and the horse's mouth should be in a straight line.

Forward Seat

Here you spare the horse's back by lifting your bottom out of the saddle and bending your upper body forward. The stirrups are shortened by two to three holes. It's critical that you find your balance and your feet are standing securely in the stirrups. The forward seat is used for trail riding and jumping. It's also good to use when training a young horse as it protects his still developing back muscles.

Enjoying a canter.

When warming up or cooling down at a walk at the beginning and end of a lesson, let the reins go long to allow your horse to stretch his neck.

Balance and Steering

Sitting up straight on horseback but not getting tense and stiff is pretty challenging because you're constantly moving with the horse. Your mind and body are busy trying to keep your balance. At the beginning, it's all about "going with the flow" with your body. Later on, you start influencing the horse in order to get him to change directions or speed. Steer using your line of sight (where you look) and the slight change of weight that comes naturally.

Even though I love riding Hobbit the most, I ride other horses every now and then during my lessons so I can gather more experience. Every horse reacts a little differently.

25

Which Horse for You?

There are so many different horses and ponies out there: small and big, young and old, calm and even a little "fiery." Which one is the best fit for you? With this quiz you can find out. Just answer all the questions and the total number of each symbol will tell you the answer. Have fun!

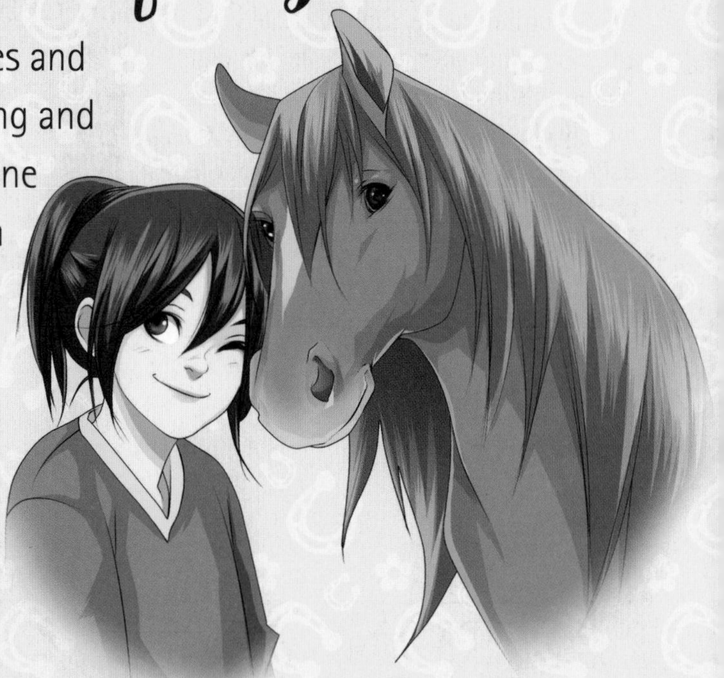

MAKE A CHART LIKE THIS TO CHECK OFF YOUR ANSWERS:

☆ | 1 2 3 4 5 | 6 7 8 9 10
♥ | 1 2 3 4 5 | 6 7 8 9 10
♘ | 1 2 3 4 5 | 6 7 8 9 10

1. How long have you been riding?

☆ I just started.

♘ A few months to a year.

♥ Since forever!

2. How often do you go to the barn?

♥ Every day.

☆ Once a week.

♘ Several times a week.

3. How often would you like to ride?

♘ Several times a week.

☆ Once a week.

♥ Every day.

4. Do you prefer big horses or ponies?

♘ The bigger the better!

☆ Ponies, for sure.

♥ Doesn't matter, as long as the horse behaves.

5. What's your favorite way to ride?

- ☆ On the longe line.
- ♥ On the trail.
- 🧲 With a group of friends.

6. When the weekend comes, what do you do?

- 🧲 Go to my riding lesson.
- ☆ Sleep in and read horse books.
- ♥ Get up early and help at the barn.

7. You wanted to ride but it started to pour...what now?

- ♥ I put on rain gear! The horses need exercise no matter what the weather is like.
- 🧲 I ride in the indoor arena.
- ☆ I skip today's lesson.

8. Your instructor assigns you a horse that is easily excited. What do you say?

- ☆ Sorry, I really can't ride him!
- 🧲 Umm...maybe next week?
- ♥ He seems fun!

9. You get some money for your birthday. What do you buy?

- ☆ A horse book or horsey decorations for my room.
- ♥ Leg wraps, a fancy halter, treats – most definitely something for my favorite horse!
- 🧲 New riding gloves or something else I need for riding.

10. Mucking stalls, feeding, sweeping, cleaning tack: What do these mean to you?

- 🧲 Strenuous, but needs to be done.
- ♥ Basically, they are my life.
- ☆ You're supposed to clean tack?

Which answer did you pick the most: ☆ , 🧲 , or ♥ ?
Here you can read what your results mean.

☆ SCHOOL HORSE

You still feel like a beginner on horseback. You have riding lessons once or twice a week. You think horses are incredibly cute, but also a little bit scary. For that reason, it does make you feel a bit better when there's someone around to help you out when you're grooming or saddling a horse. You'd rather not bother with feeding and mucking out. A sweet, well-behaved school horse or pony that's not too big and has lots of patience and experience – that's just the right thing for you!

🧲 LEASED HORSE

You've been horseback riding for a little while and are totally infected with the "horse bug." You make a lot of time to spend with your favorite horses at the barn and would love to be with them every day. So far, horse shows haven't been very important to you, but who knows what the future might hold. In your ideal horse dream, you get to visit one sweet, special horse every day, groom him and ride him, too, but someone else takes care of the mucking, feeding, and paying the veterinarian.

♥ YOUR OWN HORSE

You've been riding for just about as long as you've been walking, and no horse scares you. You enjoy riding, grooming, and caring for all horses and ponies, and already have done a little showing. And it's no wonder, because you can manage any horse, even if he's young or difficult. You would sacrifice every free minute and your allowance for a horse and are very diligent and goal-oriented. Your own horse, for which you'd carry full responsibility? No problemo – you feel fully prepared for the challenge!

The Language of Horses

I love going on walks with Hobbit and letting him graze. He lowers his head to munch on some grass, swishes his tail back and forth to keep off pesky insects, and swivels his ears in different directions.

The ears can move forward, side-to-side, or backward.

The eyes are on the sides of the head, so horses can see almost 360 degrees.

The nostrils open and close as the horse breathes.

The tongue detects the taste of food and water.

The horse detects any contact with his skin and hair - he is sensitive to even the slightest touch.

The Sensory Organs

A horse has the same sensory organs as you: eyes, nose, ears, tongue, and skin. As a prey animal, horses are constantly on the lookout for predators. Even though a domestic horse is probably not in danger of being attacked, the flight instinct is very deeply rooted. You should be patient and understanding of the fact that your horse gets spooked by things that you didn't even notice or don't find threatening at all. Horse ears are very mobile and can hear sounds coming from different directions. Since a horse's eyes are on the sides of his head, he can see more than you can without turning his head. Horses have a very keen sense of taste and smell in order to identify palatable food but also friends or potential threats. Their skin is so sensitive it notices immediately when a tiny insect lands on their coat.

What Do You See?

Horses can see almost 360 degrees with their eyes on the sides of their heads. I, on the other hand, have to turn my head to see around me. Hobbit only does this to see something clearly, as he can only do that when looking at the object with both eyes. Horses can't see all the colors that we can. They see hues of green, yellow, and blue best.

Eye Contact

A horse's gaze says a lot about his mood. In this shot, the photographer is being closely observed.

Greeting

Here, a young horse greets the alpha stallion. The stallion is in a friendly mood, as you can tell from his ears.

Scratch and Tickle

Mutual grooming is a sign of friendship or an invitation to play.

Resting

Lying down to sleep or doze off is only an option because this young horse feels safe in his herd.

Driving

A stallion drives a young horse with his head held very low and his ears back.

Leading

This stallion shows dominance by presenting himself with an open mouth and a raised tail.

Facial Expressions

Is the horse's mouth relaxed or tense? Do the eyes look friendly, fearful, or mad? Are the ears perked up or folded down close to the head? Do the nostrils look soft and blowing or narrow and wrinkled? You can learn how to read a horse's facial expressions.

Flehmen Response

The Flehmen Response allows the horse to sense certain smells using the Jacobson organ. This special sensory organ lies beneath the upper lip. Often this behavior is seen in stallions that are detecting the smell of a mare. The behavior can also indicate colic – see page 59.

Hobbit, do you like the smell of apple shampoo?

Walk, Trot, Canter

"Notice the way that Hobbit's steps feel. Just let your legs hang loose and close your eyes," says Susan. At a walk, I sway back and forth. My legs swing from left to right along Hobbit's sides. What a sweet feeling!

WALKING is a slow and comfortable four-beat gait. At any given time the horse has two or three hooves on the ground. There's minimal swinging back and forth, making it easy to stay seated. You always want to ride at a walk when warming up or cooling down the horse.

At a **TROT**, two hooves hit the ground at the same time for two beats. It's always the two legs diagonally across from one another, like the front left and hind right leg, for example. The relatively fast movement back and forth generates a lot of swinging. A posting or rising trot is the best way to ride the trot when you start riding (see page 35).

It's always been my dream to canter. It feels fantastic – almost like we're flying!

Backing Up

When horses walk backward, they step in the same manner and order as at a trot (diagonally). The front left and hind right leg step backward simultaneously, followed by the front right and hind left legs. Normally you back up about one horse-length, so three or four steps.

A Sense of Rhythm

Try out the different gaits of a horse yourself. Of course, you'll need to walk on all fours for that, though it works on two legs, as well. Walking is a measure of four beats. Just walk normally at a slow pace and count to four: one, two, three, four. Trotting is a measure of two beats. Jog, lifting your knees with each step, and count: one, two, one, two. The canter is a measure of three beats. Jump forward with one leg and take your "hind" leg with you mid-jump. Count: one, two, three, one, two, three. Counting also helps when you're riding. If you think about the rhythms when transitioning between gaits, it'll help you shift your seat and the position of your body. When slowing from a trot to a walk, count in your head, "One, two," then give the aids, breathe out, and count, "One, two, three, four." The horse will walk.

> Cantering on two legs – I can do that!

CANTER is a three-beat gait that is faster than the trot. There are two options: a left-lead or right-lead canter, where the difference lies in which legs are in front. There are brief moments of "floating" or suspension, where none of the feet are on the ground.

Some horses have **AMBLING GAITS**, special gaits they are bred for that are smooth to ride. Icelandic horses, for example, perform the tölt (a four-beat gait, like walking) and the flying pace (a two-beat gait like the trot, but lateral – that is, the legs on the same side move together).

Tölt   Flying Pace

"Sidedness" in Horses

Every horse is born with a slight laterality, or "sidedness," which can be compared to how humans are either right- or left-handed. When carrying a rider on his back, a horse's muscles and joints can be damaged over time because of this preference for or stiffness on one side or the other. An important task of a rider is to train the horse in such a way as to balance out this one-sidedness. For this, schooling exercises are quite useful. A common phrase you'll hear riding teachers say is, "Ride your horse forward and straighten him." This means that the horse has to walk energetically forward. The hind legs should step in the footsteps of the front. Only then is the horse straight – even if you are riding a turn or curve.

LOCOMOTION

Sometimes, people refer to a good canter stride as having "jump" or "jumping through." This refers to the "bounce" or loft (that "floating" suspension) when the horse's feet are off the ground.

31

How to Draw Horses

To sketch, you'll need:

- Paper
- Pencil
- Ruler
- Eraser

When I'm not at the barn I love sketching Hobbit. I've been practicing for a while, but my drawings still look pretty weird sometimes. Should I show you a few tricks that make drawing horses a lot easier? Plus, I'll give you an idea for making a horsey pencil holder - everyone needs one!

1. Horse Head from a Square

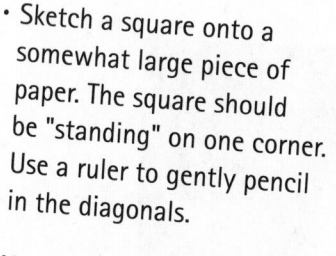

- Sketch a square onto a somewhat large piece of paper. The square should be "standing" on one corner. Use a ruler to gently pencil in the diagonals.

- Now, sketch a horse's head. The edges of the square and the diagonals are there as guides.

- Add some details, like the eye, nostril, and mouth.

- When you're done you can erase the square and diagonal lines, and color in the head.

2. A Horse from Circles

Sketch two large and one small circle. Add the legs, neck, and further details, like the ears, tail, and mane.

First three circles

Connect the circles

Draw a horse

Erase your circle guides

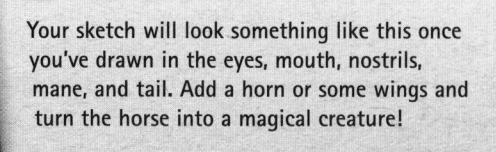
Your sketch will look something like this once you've drawn in the eyes, mouth, nostrils, mane, and tail. Add a horn or some wings and turn the horse into a magical creature!

For the pencil holder you'll need:

- An empty can
- Wavy cardboard (about 8½ x 11)
- Double-sided tape
- Scissors, pencil, and ruler
- Black felt-tip marker
- Leftover yarn
- Craft glue

3. Pencil Holder

- Measure the height and circumference of the tin can and cut a piece of wavy cardboard to fit around it.
- Tape double-sided tape onto the tin can, remove the plastic tape cover, and stick the piece of cardboard around the tin can.
- Draw a horse head onto the back of the remaining piece of cardboard, adding an extra third of an inch in length to the neck (this will be the flap to glue it onto the can).
- Cut out the horse head and place it onto the back of the remaining cardboard (with the wavy side facing up).
- Trace the outline of the horse head with a pencil, and cut it out of the cardboard. Now you have two horse heads! Add some eyes and nostrils with the felt pen and fold the flaps on each neck to the front.
- To create the mane, glue yarn pieces in between the two horse heads, then glue those together. Don't glue the flaps together – you'll need those to glue the head onto the tin can.
- Now you need to glue a tail of yarn onto the inside of the back of the can, and there! You have a pencil-holding pony!

Maxi's Tip

Does your can have sharp edges? If so, ask your parents to tape the edges. Also, with a paintbrush and some watercolors, you can turn your pencil-holding pony into a dappled horse super easily.

Learning a Balanced Seat

Close your eyes.

Does "balance" make you think of gymnastics? Well, gymnastics on horseback is super fun! There are exercises that will help you improve your balance, which is really important for you as a rider.

Training in the Saddle

Can you ride a skateboard or walk a balance beam? If so, you have a good awareness of your body! Exercises 1 through 5 on these pages will help you follow the horse's movements more closely when sitting in the saddle. Try them out on the longe line, so you can fully concentrate on your position while your riding instructor or a friend controls your horse.

On the Longe Line

To longe a horse means to "lead" him around a circle on a long rope. The "longeur" holds the longe line in whichever hand is closest to the horse's head and a whip in the other hand, closest to the hindquarters, in order to drive the horse forward. A horse that has learned to obey vocal commands to change gaits is very good at longeing.

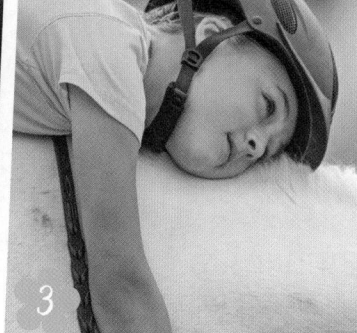

Touch your feet.

Hug the horse.

Circle your toes.

Balance a dressage whip.

1 Just try riding at a walk with your eyes closed. Can you feel how you're softly swaying from left to right?

2 Touch your left hand to your right foot, and then your right hand to your left foot. Bend down low!

3 Hug your horse. Can you reach your arms all the way around his neck?

4 Move the tips of your toes around in a circle. First, ten times around clockwise, then counter-clockwise, then switch feet. Can you also rotate both your feet at the same time, or circle them in opposite directions?

5 Balance a whip in your open hands. Try it at a walk and then a trot. Don't grip the handle!!

Seat training exercises can be practiced on a wooden horse or gymnastics horse, which spares your horse if you are just a beginning rider.

Posting or Rising Trot

As we learned, trotting is a two-beat movement, and at first it can really throw you around! By posting or rising every other step, you use the up-and-down movements of the horse to lift and lower your bottom, out of and into the saddle. At first you won't get it consistently, but when you do finally manage it a few times in a row following the horse's rhythm, it's a wonderful feeling. Eventually you'll be able to post easily and automatically. "Maxi, change your diagonal," says Susan whenever I'm in the arena and posting in time with the wrong leading step. I have to rise when Hobbit's outside front leg is striding forward and sit when it's going back.

Maxi's Tip

If you're really tense and stiff in the saddle, try humming your favorite song and smiling to drive the fear and stress away. It also helps to move your lips around, as if you're thinking really hard.

35

Riding in a Group

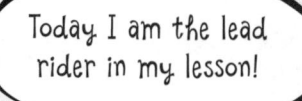

Today, I am the lead rider in my lesson!

"All right, everyone, go large around the arena at working trot! March!" Sometimes Susan seems really strict. When I ride in a group lesson, there are a lot of rules to follow. Sometimes I get to ride Hobbit in front of all the other kids though, which is fun!

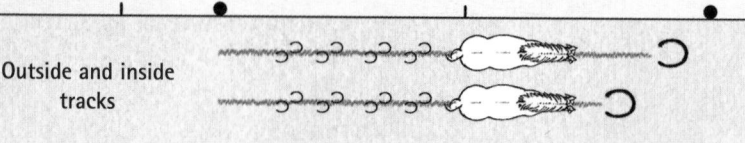

Outside and inside tracks

Tracks

In the arena, there are multiple "tracks" you can follow. Right along the fence or wall is called the outside track. There are also second and third tracks, which are further inside the outside by one horse-width each.

Like Soldiers

Riding in a group and the commands associated with it originate from times when soldiers rode on horseback. They used to form groups and ride together in big courtyards. To avoid chaos, specific riding figures were created, which everyone had to follow. Still today, riding school figures are an important part of riding education and the training of a horse. When first learning to ride, it's helpful to ride in a group because your horse will follow the one in front of him, and you can focus on your seat.

ARENA RULES

→ When you want to enter the ring with your horse, call, "Enter?" from the gate. When you hear the response, "Clear!" from others in the arena, you can enter.

→ "Left shoulder to left shoulder" is the rule for passing someone riding in the opposite direction.

→ A rider riding at a walk should leave the outside track free for riders riding at a trot or canter.

→ Those riding the whole track have the right of way over those riding circles and figure eights.

→ Halt on an inside track.

There's a saying you might have heard that goes, "You can only learn how to ride by riding." Horseback riding is a unique sport where you move in unison with another living being. You need to focus not only on your own body but also feel the horse. It takes patience and determination to get past the initial hurdles as a beginner. But that's what is so fun about horseback riding! Every lesson is a whole new experience.

Quadrille

A quadrille is a group of an even number of horses, if possible, that rides known or made-up figures all together in all three gaits. Music with a beat that works with the movements is part of it, too. It's a lot of fun, including for the horses, who do a great job participating. This kind of practice helps you because you have to concentrate on where you are and what you are riding next.

A quadrille with eight horses – not so easy!

Left or Right Rein

This denotes which direction in the arena you're riding. "Right rein" means that the middle of the arena should be on your right-hand side.

Maxi's Tip

When riding in a group, always keep one horse-length distance between you. If the speed is too slow for your horse, ride all the way into the corners; too fast, "round out" your figures toward the middle of the arena to catch up.

Handmade Horse Jewelry

Any necklace or bracelet with horses on it makes the heart of a horse lover beat a little faster! You can make fun jewelry with a horse theme yourself. Wouldn't that be a cool gift idea for your best horse-crazy friend?

For the necklace you'll need:

- Modeling clay
- Small horse figure or pendant
- Needle
- Leather cord

You can use a horse keychain, necklace charm, or an earring to imprint your mold.

1. Necklace

- Knead a piece of modeling clay until it is soft, and then knead it into a ball. Now, press the horse pendant, main side first, into the clay. Your charm should now be a thick, flat disc with a nice imprint of the horse pendant. It doesn't hurt to try it a few times until you really like how it comes out.

- Use the needle to poke a hole in the top of your clay charm. This is how you will hang it on the necklace. Make sure it's big enough for the leather cord to fit through.

- Do you want to add some beads? Roll small pieces of modeling clay into balls and poke holes through them with your needle. After you poke the holes, you need to carefully reform them so they're round, or you could end up with flat or square beads!

- After drying the clay (read the instructions on the package to find out how), string your charm and beads onto your leather cord and tie a knot to secure them.

You shouldn't wear any jewelry while you're riding. You could get it caught on something and hurt yourself!

Shrink film gets baked in the oven. In the process, it gets smaller and thicker. Take a look while it's shrinking – it looks pretty neat!

You can find great templates for horse pictures in books or horse magazines.

For the bracelet you'll need:

- Shrink film (from crafts store)
- Black felt-tip or acrylic marker
- Ruler and compass (or a round object)
- Pencil and colored pencil
- Scissors and hole punch
- Leather cord

② Bracelet

- Use a black pen to draw a 1½-inch-wide circle onto the rough side of the shrink film. You can use a compass or trace around the end of a glue stick or another round object.
- Place the circle over the picture of a horse in a book or magazine. Trace the outline with a pencil and then color the inside with a black pen. Color the rest of the circle with different colors, and then cut it out.
- Use the hole punch to punch a hole in the charm. Make several more this way.
- Now it's time for shrinking! Look at the package to find out how and ask your parents for help.
- String your charms onto the leather cord and secure them with knots.

For a really fun result, combine several different horse pictures on your charms.

Maxi's Tip

You can buy arts-and-crafts modeling clay at any store and in all sorts of colors. Even with glitter! I like to make more than just beads from it, like hearts or horseshoes. I attach these to my keychain, zippers, belt loops...

Handling on the Ground

Getting your horse can be a real challenge when turned out and standing close with others. Sometimes Hobbit won't even raise his head when I come because the grass is just too yummy.

Groundwork

A crop or dressage whip can be of great service as an extension of your arm when a horse is difficult to lead. You can hold it in your left hand and use it to drive the horse at the flank when he doesn't want to walk forward. Alternatively, you can ask a helper to walk to one side behind the horse with the crop. Even at a safe distance, her presence can help motivate the horse. The crop can also be of use when the horse gets too close or crowds you - use it to reestablish his distance. Think of the crop or whip as a type of "pointer" and not a punishing device.

Haltering

Always put the halter on from the left side because most horses are familiar with that, and the halter buckle is on the left side. Tidy up the mane and forelock after you pull the headpiece over the ears. When everything's on right, attach the snap to the ring, facing away from the horse's coat. Hold the lead rope in both hands.

Putting the halter on.

Catching the Horse

"It's really important that you are thinking good thoughts when you go out to catch a horse," says Susan. "If you're scared or unsure or angry, Hobbit will notice, even from far away. He will evade you. Ask me or an older girl for help if this happens."

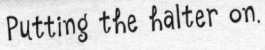

Leading Correctly

Lead your horse so that you're walking left of his head. Keep an eye on his facial expressions. Hold the lead rope in your right hand at a length that allows the horse's head and neck to be in a straight line (not curved toward you). Hold the lead rope with your right hand closer to the horse's head and your left gathering the end of the rope.

Nice, relaxed leading.

When leading a horse, it's important to stay in your own track beside him so that you don't cut him off or cause him to stop.

Even though it might seem fun to sit next to your pony, it is safer to stay on your feet at all times

CAUTION! Never wrap the lead rope around your hands, as you could really hurt yourself!

WHAT DO I DO?

Something scared Hobbit. He spooks and is ready to leap forward... what do I do?

A Stand still and talk to him in a calm voice.

B Let go of the lead rope and chase after him, yelling at him to stop.

A is correct

Maxi's Tip

Plan enough time to bring your horse in before a lesson. It can be really stressful when you try to catch him in a hurry. You can also practice in the pasture when you don't have a lesson.

School Figures

It is good to learn the basic ways of changing directions and riding different-sized circles. Boy, sometimes it feels like a lot to remember, but I'm supposed to lead the group in my lesson tomorrow so it would be super embarrassing to not know my schooling figures!

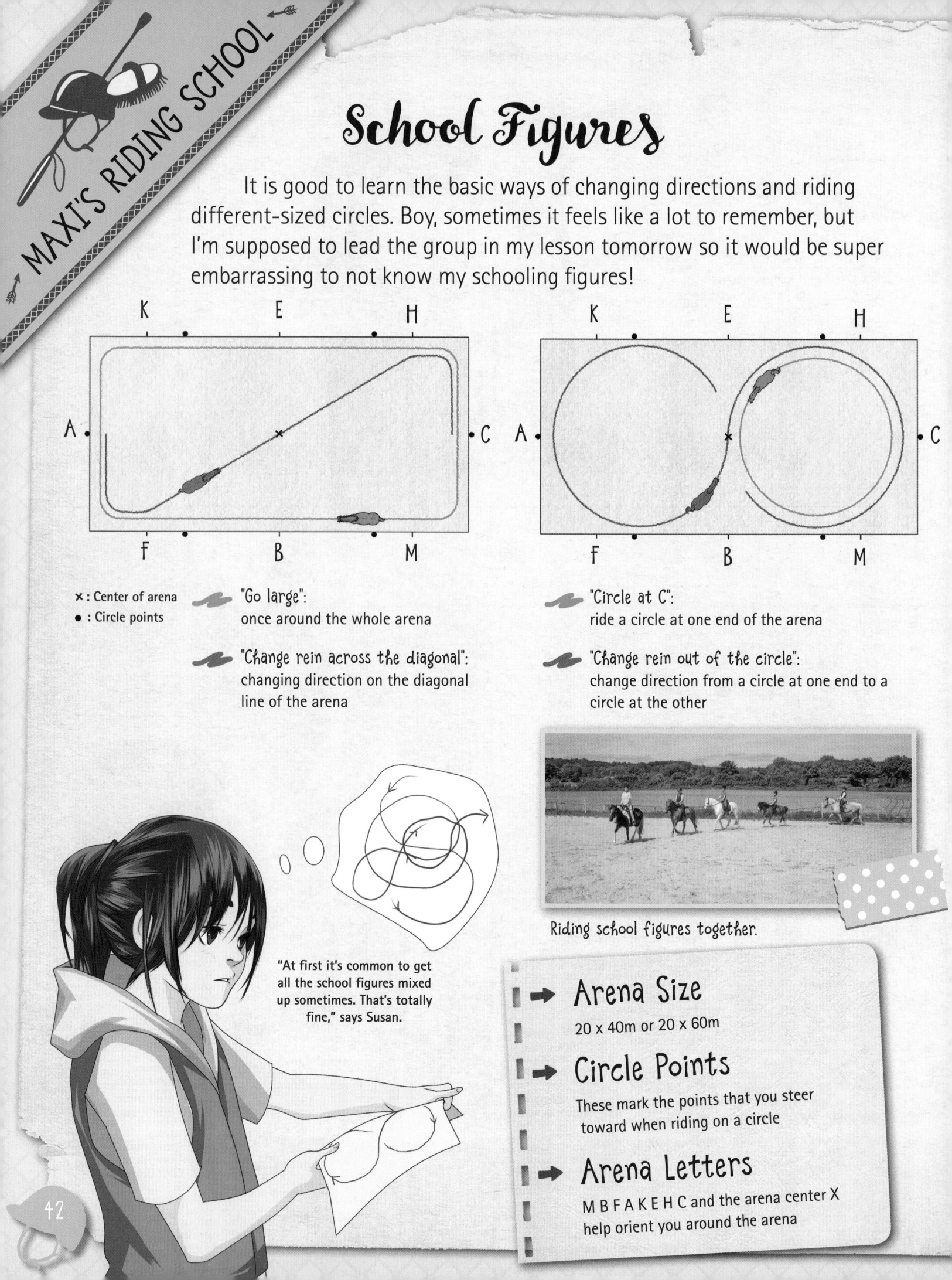

× : Center of arena
● : Circle points

"Go large":
once around the whole arena

"Change rein across the diagonal":
changing direction on the diagonal line of the arena

"Circle at C":
ride a circle at one end of the arena

"Change rein out of the circle":
change direction from a circle at one end to a circle at the other

"At first it's common to get all the school figures mixed up sometimes. That's totally fine," says Susan.

Riding school figures together.

→ Arena Size
20 x 40m or 20 x 60m

→ Circle Points
These mark the points that you steer toward when riding on a circle

→ Arena Letters
M B F A K E H C and the arena center X help orient you around the arena

42

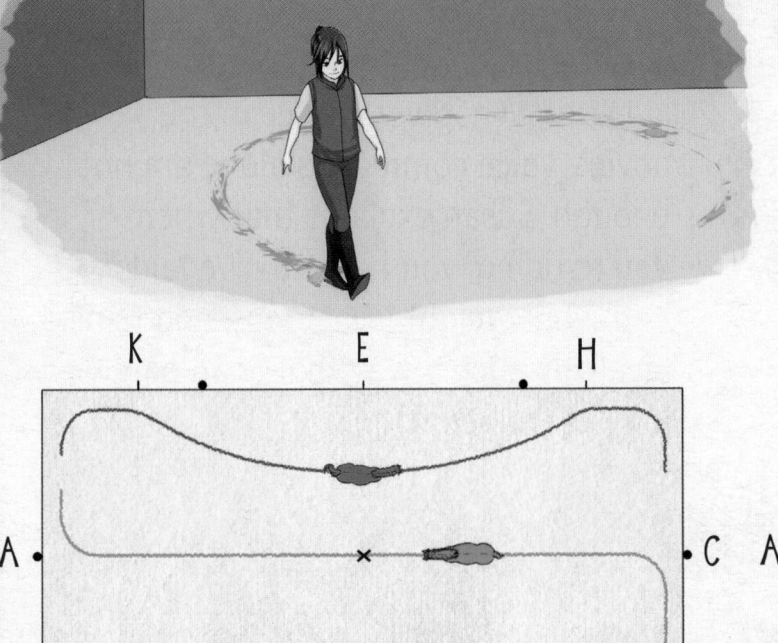

Figures of a Different Sort

Try riding the school figures differently than usual, such as "across the short diagonal": ride along the outside track until you reach the mid-point of one of the long sides (so B or E) and then ride along the diagonal and change rein.

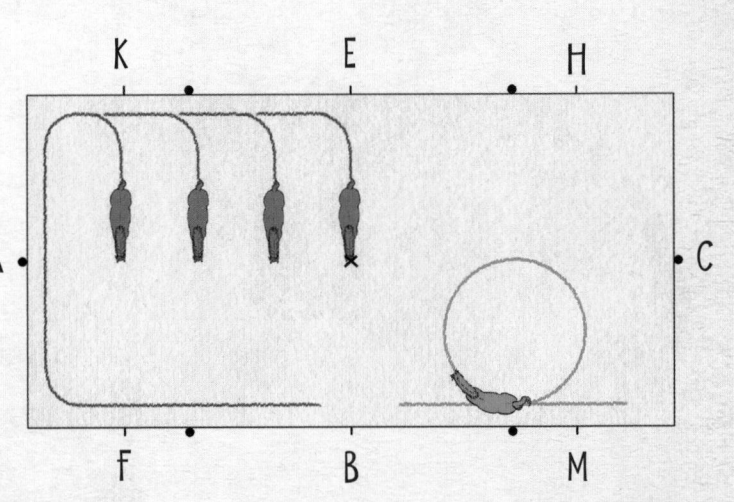

🐎 "Change directions down the centerline":
go down the middle and change directions on the short end

🐎 "Shallow serpentine":
one curve that reaches the quarter line and then returns to the rail

🐎 "Volte":
circle with 10m diameter

🐎 "Group turn right, walk on!":
in a quadrille, all riders turn simultaneously toward the center of the arena

Good Riding Practice

🎩 Regular change of gait from walk to trot to canter = practicing transitions

🎩 Changing directions frequently = equal training on both sides

🎩 Changing the speed within the same gait = shorter or longer steps

🎩 Loosen the reins every now and then for a short break = ensures suppleness

"March Up"

When practicing a quadrille, at the beginning and end of the riding lesson, the group should line up in an orderly fashion. The horses should be in a straight line and have enough distance between one another so that the riders can dismount.

Did You Know That ...

... cones are really useful to help you orient yourself around the arena. It helps the horses, too, because you have a visual goal to aim for, which helps to make your aids more clear.

Giving the Aids

"Giddy up!" Whatever we see in the movies, voice commands alone are not enough. Susan explains that when you're riding, you have to give "aids" with your weight (seat), legs, and reins. "Ideally in such a way that I can barely see what you're doing," she says.

When I look to the right, the rest of my body follows: shoulders, hips, and thighs.

10m circle.

Coming back to the outside track.

Left-Hand Turn

Leg Aids

Use your legs to drive the horse and specify the direction you want to go. Usually your lower legs drive the horse approximately where the girth is. To pick up the canter, your outer leg moves back a little bit for a second. You should only press your legs against the horse briefly and then relax them again. If you are constantly pushing with them your horse won't be able to understand what you want and might stop reacting to your aids to move forward.

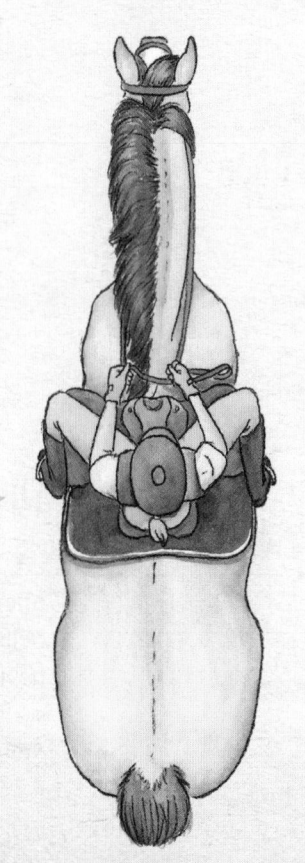

Giving aids is the interplay between weight (seat), leg, and rein, precisely coordinated and tuned to one another.

Weight Aids

This is a rider's most important aid. The horse has to stay in balance with the rider on his back, so he reacts very sensitively to every shift in the rider's weight. You can bend forward, lean backward, or turn sideways; your horse will register all three movements as signals.

The primary way to steer your horse is using your weight. He will react to any change in your seat.

Can you feel the connection to your horse's mouth?

Rein Aids

You should never pull on the reins, even if it's hard not to! Steering is accomplished with the your legs and your weight. The reins are just there to keep a soft contact with the bit in the horse's mouth. You can shorten the reins by opening your hands and then closing them on the reins again, but a bit farther up. In order not to lose the rein you are shortening, hold that rein with your opposite hand as you release.

A moment of praise!

Transitioning to walk.

Full Halt and the Half-Halt

In riding language, we call the aid for slowing down before transitioning into a slower gait a "half-halt." Slowing to a complete stop is called a "full halt." The halt is performed as follows: Pull your stomach in a bit and breathe out. In doing so, your hips will move slightly backward and the bones of your bottom will press into the saddle. Your horse will understand this as a signal to slow down. Use your legs to drive the horse forward again or to speed up.

THE CROP

The crop or whip's purpose is to reinforce your leg aids. Touch the crop to the horse's flank to drive him forward. Stop immediately as soon as he speeds up.

Maxi's Tip

Signal words, like "Trot" or "Whoa," or making a clucking or kissing noise, are called "voice aids." They aren't allowed in dressage tests, but otherwise they are very useful when communicating with your horse.

45

Falling Off

A Totally Messed-Up Riding Lesson

So, I've already been going to riding lessons for a few months now. Whenever possible, I bike to the barn in the afternoon to help out. By now, I'm a real expert at mucking out! As a reward, Susan lets me participate in another riding lesson once or twice a week. Of course, I can't always ride Hobbit, but Tapir, Flummy, Rabanus, and the other school ponies are really sweet. Hobbit's still my favorite, though! He always looks at me curiously when I'm walking toward his stall. I often bring him a carrot, pet him, and just stay and talk to him when there is time.

But today, everything wasn't good from the start. It was total chaos at home. My mom demanded I clean my room and play with Leo. I was super late getting to the barn; everyone else was already entering the arena! I had to get Hobbit ready really quickly: clean his hooves, brush the saddle area, and fetch the saddle and bridle.

However, Hobbit really wasn't in the mood for such a rushed job. He held his head so high that I couldn't get his bridle on him.

"C'mon, Hobbit!" I scolded, putting the saddle on first. I really didn't want to hurt him, I swear! But I think I was in such a rush that I really just heaved the saddle onto his back and tightened the girth too tight right away. He huffed at me and rolled his eyes! Somehow, I was able to get my hand over his nose and bridle him, even though he really didn't want to open his mouth for the bit. I had to reprimand him over and over again, and we both ended up in a bad mood.

In the arena we pulled ourselves together. We lined up with the group and prepared to give it our best.

"Trot!," called Susan while I was leading the other riders in the group. And then, "Extended trot!"

Hobbit really doesn't like to lead in the lessons. He'd much rather follow the others. And after already arriving late to the lesson, I really didn't want to embarrass myself again. So I drove Hobbit like crazy with my legs. But he trotted about as fast as a lame grandma elephant.

"Don't fall asleep, Maxi and Hobbit!" yelled Susan. Tanya giggled, and I turned bright red. So I kept driving, driving with my legs. Hobbit sped up a little bit, but it was totally impossible for me to ride an extended trot and to drive him at the same time. So instead of posting I did sitting trot, and Susan furrowed her brow.

"Extended trot, and I mean everyone!" she announced again in a strict voice.

Hobbit just slowed down again,

And then we were supposed to canter. So that we didn't go at a snail's pace again, I gave Hobbit really strong aids - and he took off like a rocketship! I was taken totally by surprise and didn't have a good seat. Then all of a sudden, Hobbit slammed to a halt, and I flew in a high arc over his head and into the sand. I didn't hurt myself at all, but the whole thing definitely was pretty embarrassing! I just sat there in shock. It was becoming crystal-clear to me why all of this had happened. I must have totally confused Hobbit by speed-grooming him, yelling at him, rushing, and ramming my legs into his sides. Maybe I even hurt him! Susan had a hold of Hobbit's reins as she came to me.

"Hey, Maxi. It's okay. We all make mistakes sometimes," she said.

And my dear Hobbit? He lowered his head and huffed through his nose, as if he wanted to say, "Are you okay? Shall we keep going?"

"It's okay, darling," I whispered back to him. I hugged him and gave him a pat. And then I got right back on.

Pasture Life

Horses are animals of fields, flight, and herds. They only feel safe and comfortable in groups with other horses. They live the most naturally turned out with others in big pastures.

Hobbit in the Pasture

"Take a look at what the horses do all day out in the pasture," Susan suggested. At first, I thought just watching them was boring. But then I grew interested: I observed which horses grazed near one another and how often they pooped, drank, or rolled around. Try it! Figure out which horse is the "boss" of the herd and which horses are friends. How can you tell? Other horses will voluntarily get out of the way of the alpha horse, for example if it's about getting a good spot at the water trough or hay pile. Horses that are friends will seek bodily contact with one another, grooming each other, sometimes lining up head-to-tail next to each other in order to swish away pesky insects.

What does Hobbit do all day long without me?

Walking

Wild horses usually move at a walk. It's their most natural gait and requires the least energy. When a horse is grazing, he moves at a walk from one patch of grass to another. At a trot or canter, he holds his head higher in order to be able to observe his surroundings.

Grazing

Horses that live in the wild spend nearly 20 hours a day grazing. They aren't ruminants, like cows. Horses eat about 2.2lbs of hay an hour, and they can eat about as much when they graze. They bite off blades of grass with their front teeth and grind them with their back teeth. The noise that they make while doing so is quite calming, so listen up!

Napping and Sleeping

Horses only sleep about three hours a day, usually deep in the night and for short periods of time - about 30 minutes each. Horses usually nap and sleep standing up. They barely close their eyes and rest one hind leg, then the other. The only time they lie down to sleep is when they feel very safe.

Horses often scratch themselves – for example, when insects are bothering them or they are in the middle shedding their winter coat. They might rub their nose against their leg, like the horse in this picture, or they scratch themselves on a tree branch, or they roll around in the dirt. Whatever it takes, as long as the itching stops!

Playing and Grooming

Horses form friendships, too. They get along splendidly with some of their kind, and less so with others, but they still respect one another – just like with humans. Playing together or mutual grooming is a sign of true friendship.

Horses drink very carefully: they dip their lips in the water and suck the water through them. Listen to a horse drinking, or try it out yourself. It's similar to drinking with a straw.

I can drink like a horse!

Homemade Horse Treats

I asked Susan if I can feed Hobbit homemade horsie treats (the answer was I may!). I have a recipe that is super easy to bake and has lots of healthy ingredients. Hobbit loves my treats! And to store them I crafted a cookie jar, using an empty can and recycled wrapping paper from my last birthday.

> Careful! Don't feed the treats to your horse until three days after you've baked them. Before then they're too fresh.

For the treats you'll need:

- 3 large apples
- 10 bags of fennel tea
- 4 cups coarse oatmeal
- 4 cups cornflakes
- 2 cups whole wheat flour
- 1 cup oil
- 1 mixing bowl
- Grater and scissors
- Spatula
- Parchment paper and baking tray

1. The Recipe

- Ask your parents to coarsely grate the apples for you (with the peel but without the seeds).
- Cut open the tea bags and pour the contents into the large bowl along with the rest of the ingredients.
- Knead everything together with your hands.
- Put the parchment paper onto the baking tray and spread the dough onto it in one continuous layer using the spatula.
- Bake your treats at 300 degrees F for 60 to 70 minutes, until they are golden brown and crispy. Break them into pieces (each about as big as an apple slice) while they're still warm.

For the cookie jar
you'll need:

- An empty can with a lid
- White craft glue
- Wrapping paper scraps
- Tablespoon and small bowl
- Paintbrush and scissors

2. The Cookie Jar

- Rip the wrapping paper into scraps if it isn't already.
- Pour one tablespoon each of glue and water into the bowl and mix them together with the paintbrush.
- Paint the outside of the can with the glue mixture, then cover it with the scraps of wrapping paper. Paint over those with glue as well so that they stick flat to the can. Cover the whole can in this manner. Don't worry, the white shine from the glue will disappear when it dries!
- Cut off any edges that are sticking out at the top or bottom. Don't forget to wash out the brush and the bowl thoroughly!

Of course you can also decorate the lid of the can. That's best done with a paint pen or acrylic pen. You can label the lid with what's inside the can, draw patterns, or think of your own creative ideas.

An aluminum can with a plastic lid works best. Often coffee and hot cocoa are sold in cans like that. Take a look around the grocery store! ♥

Maxi's Tip

Here's a sweet surprise: mash up a banana and add oatmeal, then spread that onto an apple after removing the seeds. Don't feed this too your horse too often, though - bananas have tons of sugar.

Stable Management

"You stink!" My brothers always wrinkle their noses when I get home after horseback riding. Me, on the other hand, I love that stable smell. I never thought mucking out stalls could be so much fun.

Tools of the trade: shovel, pitchfork, and broom.

Order Must Prevail!

Susan takes great care that all the grooming tools, saddles, and bridles are put away properly. The saddles go neatly on racks attached to the wall of the tack room. Bridles and halters hang from hooks that are labeled with the names of the horses to which they belong.

♪♪♪
"...sit up straight, light rein contact, and heels down..."

SWEEPING DUTY

"Use a watering can to wet the aisle so it doesn't get so dusty when you sweep," says Susan. Fine dust takes hours to settle back down to the ground. Dusty air isn't healthy for human or horse lungs.

Horses and humans both can have allergic reactions to grass pollen or mold spores from hay. Water binds dust, so dampening the ground before sweeping helps improve the air quality in the barn.

The areas of the saddle that come in contact with your clothing should be cleaned with a sponge but not conditioned.

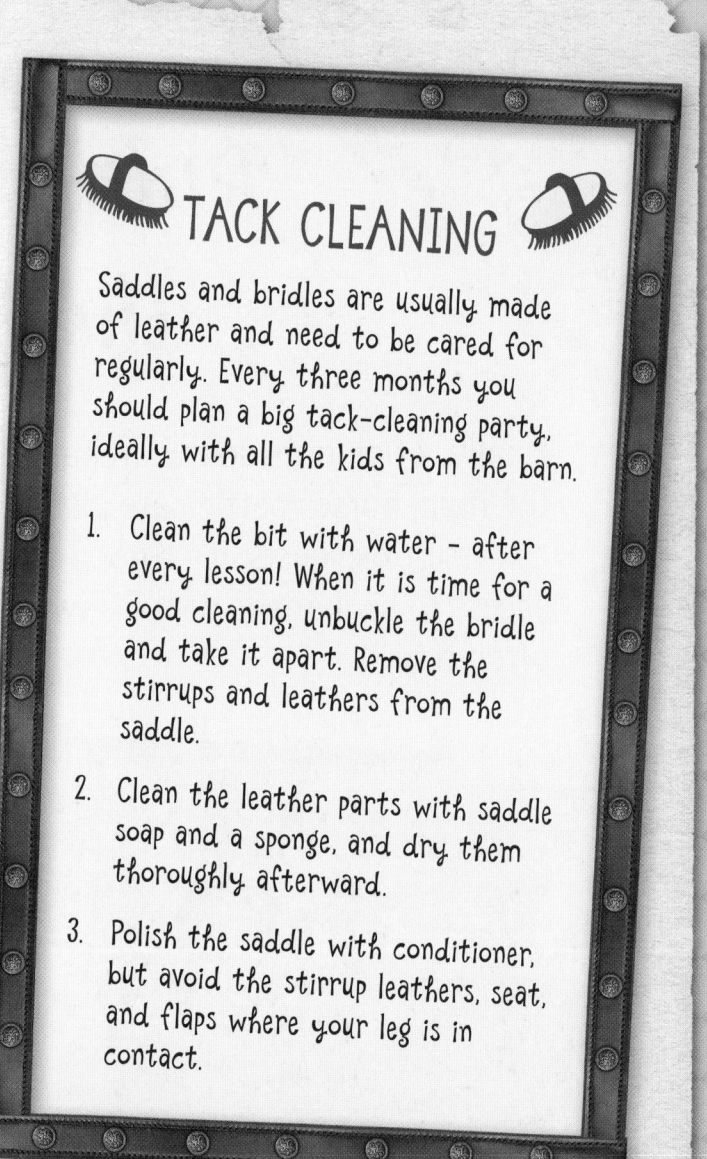

TACK CLEANING

Saddles and bridles are usually made of leather and need to be cared for regularly. Every three months you should plan a big tack-cleaning party, ideally with all the kids from the barn.

1. Clean the bit with water - after every lesson! When it is time for a good cleaning, unbuckle the bridle and take it apart. Remove the stirrups and leathers from the saddle.

2. Clean the leather parts with saddle soap and a sponge, and dry them thoroughly afterward.

3. Polish the saddle with conditioner, but avoid the stirrup leathers, seat, and flaps where your leg is in contact.

Run-In Shed

This is a run-in shed and paddock at the barn. The ponies turned out there have a free-choice shelter. They can go under the roof if the sun is blazing down or it is raining or snowing. The paddock isn't grassy. The ground is covered with a synthetic footing so that it doesn't get too deep or muddy.

Horses in the paddock.

Hey there, sunshine! Come on out and I'll clean your stall!

Box Stalls

The stalls at the barn are bedded with either straw or wood shavings so that the horses can lie down. This bedding also absorbs urine. The wet bedding and horse poop should be cleaned out daily.

Riding on the Road

Finally, a ride outside the arena! When riding down the road, horses participate just as much in traffic as cars or bicyclists. It's a good thing to have access to back roads or trails where cars don't often travel.

When hacking outside the arena with others, always keep a horse-length's distance between each other.

Trail Conditions

Some trails are just for horses and their riders. However, even if it's a riding path, you have to assess the trail conditions for yourself. You can only trot or canter when the trail isn't too muddy, too hard, too slippery, or too dusty.

In the Dark

Horses can see better at twilight than we can. An evening ride is something really special. Reflective clothing and head lamps for horses and riders are an absolute must.

Take It Easy!

On the trail, you should always ride in a way that spares the horse's back. Lengthen the stirrups by two to three holes. Trotting should always be relaxed and easy, and your diagonal should be switched regularly. Your speed has to be adjusted to other horses, your fellow riders, nearby pedestrians, and the trail conditions. Remember that even a trail ride at a walk is a wonderful adventure for both you and your horse!

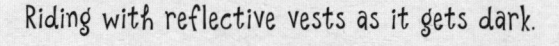
Riding with reflective vests as it gets dark.

Hand signal: "Stop."

Practice standing still while others ride ahead a short distance. Then follow at a calm walk.

Rules of a Group

When hacking with others, the group should be led and secured at the end by horse-and-rider pairs that can stay calm in stressful situations. When the trail is wide enough, two riders can ride next to one another. If you must cross a road, it is best to do so all at once as a group, in a calm and efficient manner.

Remember: keep one horse-width's of distance between one another when riding side by side.

No Riding Allowed

In some places, riding is not permitted. For example, highways are marked as places where horses cannot be ridden. Some fields and trails are posted as private where trespassing is not allowed. In some natural and protected areas, only designated trails are open to horseback riding. Respect roads and trails as marked.

Riding a bike uses some of the same aids as riding a horse: keep your eyes on where you're headed, and when you turn, your upper body turns in that direction, as well.

SIGNAGE
Pay attention to how roads and trails are marked.

Sometimes horses are allowed, sometimes not.

Dream Come True

With Sun, Mosquitoes, and Sore Muscles

I was almost as excited for this day as I was for my very first riding lesson! Today we got to go out for a ride for the first time in the fields behind the stable – almost exactly like in my dreams! Susan had already promised weeks ago that we'd get to go out on a trail ride soon. When the day we were supposed to go finally rolled around, it was absolutely perfect weather. The sun was shining, there wasn't a cloud in the sky, and all I wanted was to have the wind blow through my hair as I cantered along on horseback! But Susan put a damper on that really quickly. "Sorry, kids, but it's not going to work out today," she said. Everyone groaned.

"Why not, with all this sunshine?" I asked.

"The wind is too strong," said Susan. "It makes the horses spooky, and we really don't need that on your first trail ride."

"Grownups are always such know-it-alls," Lissy whispered to me, and I had to giggle. Lissy is super funny!

From then on I kept a close eye on the weather report. For the next riding lesson it was sunny with no wind. All clear for a trail ride! First, we tightened our girths and adjusted our stirrups. Susan lined us up in pairs. I was at the very back with Lissy – only Susan was going to ride behind us. "Elena is joining us today and riding up front," she explained. "Everyone else stays in line. If you pass Elena, you have to bake a cake for everyone as punishment." We all laughed at that. Finally we were off, at a leisurely walk away from the stable, down the road, and onto a path along a field. For a while, no one said a word. I think everyone was really enjoying how it felt to not be confined within the walls of an arena.

Soon we trotted for a little bit, which worked pretty well. And then Susan gave the command to start cantering. I got a little bit nervous that Hobbit would just take off, that I'd fall, and that Susan would yell at me again. But I barely had any time to worry. Lissy and Tapir transitioned into a canter next to me, I gave the aids and Hobbit picked it up smoothly. As if he sensed my concerns, he cantered slowly and obediently, staying right next to his friend Tapir. Wow! So there it was: the real "life on the trail" experience! It was exactly as I'd always dreamed it.

All of us were just as out of breath as our horses when we finally slowed back down to a walk. Elena guided us to a resting spot in the woods. We dismounted and tied up our ponies. "Picnic!" announced Susan, handing out granola bars and water bottles for everyone. The horses drank water from a little stream. It was so beautiful, but I was totally exhausted. I let myself fall flat in the grass, and Lissy sat down next to me. Flies and mosquitoes flew over from the stream and buzzed around us and the horses.

"Going for a trail ride is so great!" said Lissy.

"Heavenly," I replied.

"I never want to do anything else!" she said.

"Me neither!" I agreed. "I just want to ride, ride, ride, all the way to the horizon."

"Til the end of the world!" she added. Then we were silent for a while, and I rubbed my thighs. They really hurt. Lissy caught a mosquito with one big clap. "But that'd get really tiring for the ponies," I drawled.

"Yeah, you're right," said Lissy. "We can't do that to them."

We looked at each other and both started cracking up. "Everything hurts!," gasped Lissy.

"I know, me too," I said, giggling. "I couldn't care less right now about the horizon!"

Now I have two good friends at the barn: Hobbit and Lissy!

Feast Fit for a Horse

Grass, hay, minerals and vitamins, grain, apples, carrots – what do horses need in their diet to live? Susan explained to me that the composition and amount of a horse or pony's feed depends on how hard he works.

Types of Horse Feed

Horses are vegetarians. They nourish themselves mostly from roughage, meaning grasses. They eat either fresh grasses and herbs in the pasture, or dried in the form of hay in stalls and paddocks. Straw is also a kind of roughage, but it is used as bedding because it is devoid of nutrients. Concentrated feed can be made up of oats, grains, and minerals. Carrots, apples, and beets (fed in the form of pulp) shouldn't be overfed.

Water

Horses drink much more water than us – between 6.5 and 11 gallons a day. They need it in order to produce enough saliva. The drier the food they eat, the more water they need in order to swallow and digest it. In addition, when it's hot out, a horse's whole body sweats, which also requires a lot of water. Horses on free-range pasture often absorb a lot of water through the grass they eat.

Salt or Mineral Lick

Horses need minerals. They absorb some from their food, but it's also important to provide a salt or mineral "licking block" where they can help themselves when they need it. Horses kept on free-range pasture need this, too.

Free-choice hay provided on the opposite side of the fence so no horses will trample or poop on it.

In the spring, horses can only eat a little bit of grass if they were only fed hay during winter months. Their digestive system has to slowly adjust.

Mineral lick.

WHICH BELONG TOGETHER?
Match Them Up!

1.

Pellets

2.

9.

Carrots

Hay

8.

Apples

Straw

Grass

3.

Oats

7.

Grains

Herbs

6.

4.

5.

Answers: Hay & Roughage 🍀 Grass & Roughage 🍀 Carrots 🍀 Oats 🍀 Pellets 🍀 Apples 🍀 Straw Bedding 🍀 Herbs & Roughage 🍀 Grains

Treats

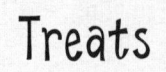

There are so many different types of treats: apples, carrots, homemade cookies (see page 50), store-bought treats. Why? You can use food to reward horses when they do something correctly. You can win a horse's trust when you greet him or say thank you after a riding lesson with a treat. Some trainers and barns don't allow feeding horses treats because they're concerned they could get pushy and nippy. Always ask first!

Colic

When a horse has a stomachache, it's called "colic." This applies to anything from a little bit of discomfort to life-threatening trouble in the intestines. Horses express pain through their body language: they look at their stomachs, have a worried or tense facial expression, lie down and roll around, or even groan sometimes. Their behavior is completely different from what you're used to seeing. If you see any of these signs, let a knowledgeable adult know right away so a veterinarian can be called.

Jumping

"I want your riding education to be as well-rounded as possible," says Susan. "There was a time when jumps were part of every dressage test." I can't wait to finally jump! I hope Hobbit sees it the same way.

Poles

Riding over a single pole at a walk – that's the beginning. I remember the first time Susan laid out three ground poles in the arena for the first time. "Straight across!" she said was the first task. We were supposed to trot with our seat raised out of the saddle and off the horse's back when he crossed the poles. At a canter, riding over the poles is even more fun.

1. This is how you go over several poles in a curved line at a trot.

2. When jumping and cantering, ride in a forward seat.

GROUND POLE DISTANCES

Gait:	Ponies	Horses
Walk:	2 ft	2½ ft
Trot:	3 ft	4 ft
Canter:	9 ft	11½ ft

Up and Down

"Today we're going to ride in the jumping arena," says Susan, and my heart skips a beat. "At a walk over the bank. Maxi, you first!" Hobbit perked up his ears and almost started trotting. So I pulled in my bellybutton and let out a deep breath. "Sloooow, Hobbit." Then we trotted over the bank, and later we cantered up the steps. So cool! "Now you guys are ready to jump cavalletti," says Susan.

When riding up and down banks and steps, you learn to balance yourself, which is great preparation for jumping.

Cavalletti

These are very practical small obstacles made of one pole and two crosses, one at either end. You can set cavalletti either so the pole lies flat on the ground, or so that it is about 12 inches off the ground. To facilitate the jump for your horse, lift your seat out of the saddle right before the obstacle and move your hands forward on either side of his neck. Two to four cavalletti can be combined in a row, either in a straight or curved line. The distances between each are the same as for ground poles.

The horse's legs should always be protected with boots or wraps when jumping in case they hit a fence.

On the Course

A jumping course is made up of several different obstacles that have to be cleared in a certain order. There are single jumps and also combinations of several obstacles.

Verticals, Oxers, Combinations

Simple jumps with a pole or poles straight across are called verticals. The horse has to jump high and not necessarily wide. Oxers are wider – two sets of standards with poles are set up, one right behind the other, so the horse has to jump high and long to clear them.

When two or three obstacles are set up in a row, with one or two cantering steps between each, it is called a "combination."

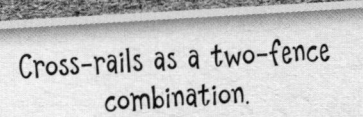

Cross-rails as a two-fence combination.

Do You Understand Your Horse?

Wouldn't it be great if Hobbit could just tell me what he wants? "Leave me alone!" or, "Yeah, rubbing me right there is perfect!" But of course that's not how it works. Fortunately Hobbit can show me what he's thinking and feeling: with his body language. For example, he might move his ears around attentively, sniff me curiously, or turn away. Do you already know how to "speak horse"?

1. A horse looks at you and turns his ears forward. What does that mean?

a	He doesn't want the wind blowing in his ears.
b	He finds you interesting.
c	He is scared.

2. Your horse pins his ears flat, pulls the corners of his mouth down, and his nostrils narrow. What do you do?

a	Keep my distance because he's threatening me.
b	Call for help because he's sick.
c	Come closer because he's happy.

3. How do you talk to horses?

a	A whisper is best.
b	Loudly; yell if you need to.
c	In a low, calm voice.

4. While you are riding, your horse swishes his tail around intensely. What does it mean?

a	He's waving away a fart.
b	He's unhappy.
c	He's greeting a friend.

Distribution of Points

1a = 0	1b = 3	1c = 0	2a = 3	2b = 0	2c = 0	3a = 0	3b = 0	3c = 3	4a = 0	4b = 3	4c = 0
5a = 3	5b = 0	5c = 0	6a = 0	6b = 0	6c = 3	7a = 3	7b = 0	7c = 0	8a = 0	8b = 3	8c = 0
9a = 3	9b = 0	9c = 0	10a = 0	10b = 0	10c = 3

5. Two horses turned out together are nibbling at each other's mane and coat. Why?

a | They like each other and are showing it.

b | Horse hair is tasty.

c | They don't get along and are trying to hurt each other.

6. What reminds horses of their mothers?

a | Patting them on the croup.

b | Pushing them to one side.

c | Placing your arm over the neck and petting the other side of it.

7. How do horses live together in a herd?

a | The hierarchy forms based on the horses' strength and experience.

b | All the animals are equal.

c | Apart from the stallion, all herd members are equal.

8. A horse pushes you away. What is he trying to say?

a | "Let's go!"

b | "Get out of my way!"

c | "I like you!"

9. Which horse is relaxed?

a   b   c

10. You arrive at your riding lesson anxious, sad, or upset. What now?

a | Doesn't matter; my horse won't notice.

b | If I really pull myself together and hide it well, it will be fine.

c | My horse can sense my mood and will react to it. Best to calm down beforehand!

How many points did you collect with your answers?
Read below to see what your results mean.

0-10 POINTS: UNDERSTANDING "HORSE SPEAK" TAKES PRACTICE!

☆

Perhaps you just started learning "horse speak" and haven't quite mastered the language yet. No problem! Take a little time before and after every riding lesson. Stay at the barn and observe the horses. It's especially interesting when they talk to one another from stall to stall. When they are turned out, you can sit for a little while at the edge of the pasture. Try to figure out what the sounds, posture, and behavior of the horses mean.

11-20 POINTS: YOU ALREADY UNDERSTAND HORSES PRETTY WELL!

☆

You have a pretty good intuition when it comes to the horse's language, and you know a few important things about it. However, you have more to learn in order to get along with horses and ponies in the best ways possible. Don't be afraid to ask your riding teacher or other experienced riders for advice. They can give you some great tips, like this one, for example: Rub your favorite horse at the withers. Horse friends nibble on each other in a similar way.

21-30 POINTS: YOU'VE MASTERED THE HORSE'S LANGUAGE!

☆

You're becoming a real "horse whisperer"! You have a sharp understanding of what the animals want to say with their body language and noises, and you can communicate well with them. Keep an eye out for clinics on horsemanship in your area. A few of these may help you learn even more ways to read horses from professionals. Definitely keep doing what you're doing! Always take your time to observe horses and their behavior.

Pasture Duty

"Off to the pasture, girls!" Susan is up front pushing the wheelbarrow, and we're trotting along behind her carrying the pitchforks. It's hot out but the pastures still have to be picked out. Afterward, we get ice cream!

Collect the piles ...

... until the wheelbarrow is full.

As Natural as Possible

Why is it so important that horses spend time out in the pasture? There are many reasons. It's healthy for horses to consume grasses while slowly grazing throughout the day. (There are, of course, some exceptions, such as breeds that originate from barren lands like Iceland, Shetland, or Norway, or those with certain health or weight issues. Pasture grasses may actually be too nutritious for these animals, so they shouldn't be allowed to graze without limits.) Horses need a lot of fresh air and should be able to move about freely in the pasture. Being able to socialize with others of their kind so they can play with or groom each other is an important part of a healthy lifestyle.

CLEANING UP OUTSIDE

When manure is left in paddocks or pastures, grass that horses won't eat grows under the piles. Also, parasites can spread more easily. To clean up paddocks and pastures, take a pitchfork or a shovel and a rake. Collect the manure in a wheelbarrow or bucket and dump it on the barn manure pile. Sometimes farmers like to work horse manure into their fields as fertilizer. If mixed with yard waste, horse droppings can also be composted and used in your own yard or garden.

Fence Patrol

Pastures should be enclosed by safe fencing in good repair, such as that made of wood or well-strung electric tape or wire. Regularly checking the fence is important in case a rail is down or the electric isn't working. I once accidentally touched the wire, and wow! An electric shock like that is not dangerous, but it definitely feels pretty nasty.

64

POISONOUS AND SAFE VEGETATION

POISONOUS

- Yew
- Red Maple
- Hemlock
- Boxwood
- Water Hemlock

POISONOUS

- Tansy Ragwort
- Foxglove
- Johnsongrass (Sudan Grass)
- Locoweed
- Ragwort
- St. John's Wort
- Lily of the Valley
- Oleander
- Marsh Marigold
- Bracken Fern

SAFE

- Stinging Nettle
- Comfrey
- Chamomile
- Dandelion
- Peppermint
- Ribwort
- Yarrow

St. John's wort is common at forest edges or around the edges of bushes.

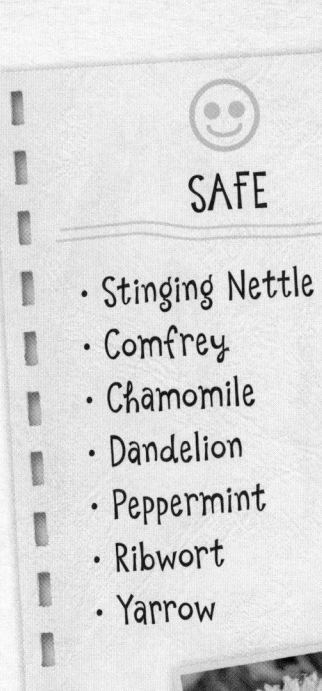

You're probably already familiar with dandelions!

DID YOU KNOW?

Horses poop up to 12 times a day. Depending on their feed, that means up to 44lbs of manure to scoop! About 20 hours pass from the time they swallow their food to the time they excrete it. Horses produce 0.8 to 2.6 gallons of urine a day and pee several times, spreading their hind legs behind them.

This fly sheet prevents insects from biting.

These flies are super annoying!!

Insect Protection

Insects are a real plague to horses in the summer: biting midges, horseflies, mosquitoes, and deerflies are common, annoying horses around the eyes, legs, and in the ears. Fly masks that cover the horse's head and sheets that protect his whole body help a lot. Blankets with black-and-white zebra stripes have recently become popular: Insects are irritated by the stripes and avoid the horses and ponies instead of landing on them. Insect repellent sprayed onto the coat also helps to keep insects away.

Knowing Horse Breeds

Lipizzaner or Lusitano? Quarter Horse or Morgan? Hanoverian or Thoroughbred? Welsh or Shetland? My book of horse breeds has over 280 breeds listed! I can't decide on a favorite one.

Have you heard of Pippi Longstocking? Her horse was called Big Uncle! He was a Knabstrupper from Denmark.

1. Warmblood

Warmbloods originated in Europe and can come from a number of bloodlines. They have naturally athletic gaits and movement, are willing to work, and are bred for a variety of equestrian disciplines.

2. Hotblood

Hot-blooded horses are some of the fastest horses on Earth, making them common choices for flat racing, steeple chasing, and endurance. They include Arabians, American Thoroughbreds, English Thoroughbreds, and Andalusians.

3. Coldblood

Coldblooded equines don't have cooler blood than other horses, they are just large, heavy breeds often used as work horses. "Cold" refers to their calmer and "less heated" temperament when compared to warmbloods and hotbloods. Some coldblood breeds are popular nowadays among recreational riders.

4. Pony

Ponies are horses that are smaller than 14.2 hands. Many pony breeds are used for competitive riding because they are just as versatile as larger horses. Popular breeds include Shetland Ponies, Connemara Ponies, and Welsh Ponies. Ponies are usually very hardy and need less food than full-sized breeds.

Big and little: The Shetland almost reaches this Warmblood's belly!

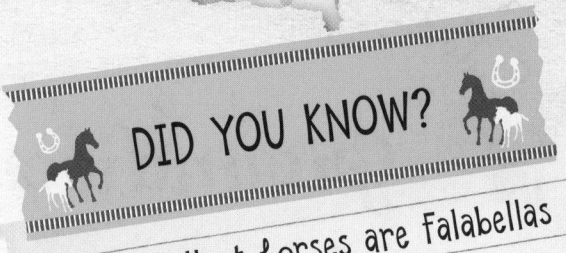
A FEW OTHER HORSE BREEDS:

Paint Horse

Lipizzaner

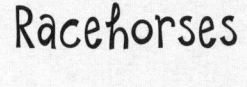
Lusitano

Racehorses

Horse racing is all about who gets around the track or course the fastest. Thoroughbreds gallop around an oval track usually for 5 to 12 furlongs. (A furlong is 220 yards.) The horses are ridden by jockeys that "float" above their mounts with really short stirrups. One of the most famous racehorses was Man o' War, considered by many to be the greatest Thoroughbred of all time. Standardbred racehorses pull light carriages called sulkies.

Groundwork

Leading, longeing, obstacle training, round pen lessons, trick training – these are all different kinds of groundwork. During school vacation I like to practice obstacle training with Hobbit using a halter, lead rope, and dressage whip.

Longeing

You've probably seen a horse move on a circle around a person on a long line before. That is called longeing; some barns have round pens and arenas just for this practice. Often, longeing is used to teach young horses to grow accustomed to the saddle and to obey voice commands. The horse is longed in the equestrian sport of vaulting.

Trotting on the longe line.

Work in Hand

Stay calm, Hobbit. We can do it!.

This means leading a horse with a bridle or cavesson, asking for certain movements as you walk or jog next to him. The horse learns lessons that are later used under saddle, as well. It's easier for horses to understand difficult dressage movements, like piaffe or passage, without the weight of a rider. They've been doing this for hundreds of years at the Spanish Riding School in Vienna.

Hobbit is willing to walk through the curtain with me. This is a great exercise for promoting trust and calmness.

Stopping the horse, using the whip.

LABYRINTH AND TARP

Some simple ideas for desensitizing the horse to scary situations include leading him through a path defined by ground poles (in an L shape or in a labyrinth). Start at a walk forward, then try backing through it. Also try walking straight across the poles. Trust is key when walking over a tarp. This is great preparation for riding through water or other changes of footing.

Desensitizing

Since horses are flight animals, many things scare them that we find totally normal. However, horses can learn to translate flight reactions into other behaviors. That means learning to walk calmly past the tractor instead of bolting off. A calm, trustworthy horse is great for kids and beginners since they aren't so confident in the saddle yet.

Ground-Pole Training

You can walk across ground poles at a walk, use them to define a simple pathway (forward and backward), or try it at a trot with more distance between the poles (see page 60).

The L

You can head forward or backward through the L made of four ground poles. Your pony should walk slowly, step by step, around the corner. A dressage whip might be useful to help maintain a certain direction and speed. Use the whip like an extension of your arm. To start walking, point the whip forward. To stop the horse, touch the whip lightly against his chest.

The Labyrinth

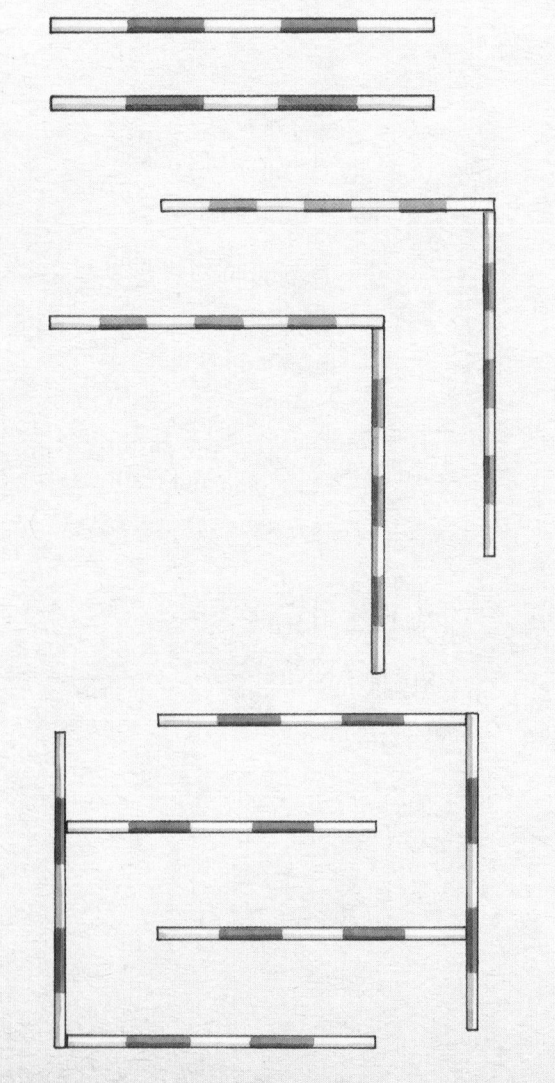

Six ground poles form a labyrinth to move through with two tight turns. Use both entrances. You can also walk your horse over the poles, rather than through the spaces between them. The labyrinth under saddle is mostly for more advanced riders. It allows the rider to fine-tune aid-giving and improves the communication between human and horse in a playful way.

Pretty heavy! Poles made of wood won't roll away so easily, even if a hoof knocks against them.

What Type of Rider Are You?

I often dream with my eyes wide open. I'm riding Hobbit in a Western saddle, I have a sleeping bag strapped behind me, and in front of me is the wide expanse of the prairie. On the other hand, my friend Lissy loves white gloves, black jackets, and riding dressage in the arena. We're just super different types of riders! How about you? Answer these questions to find out!

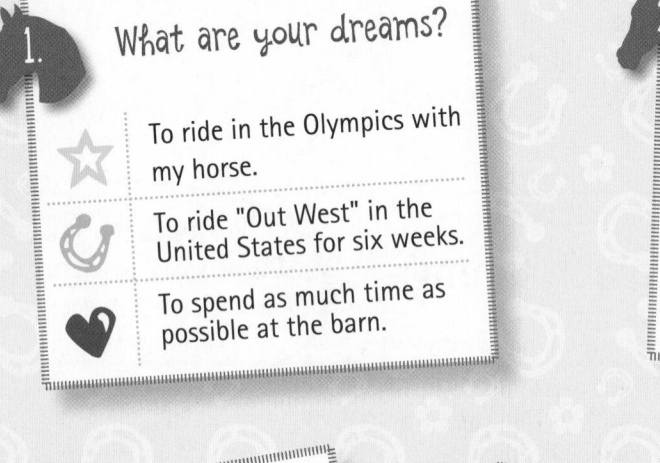

1. What are your dreams?

☆ To ride in the Olympics with my horse.

🐎 To ride "Out West" in the United States for six weeks.

❤ To spend as much time as possible at the barn.

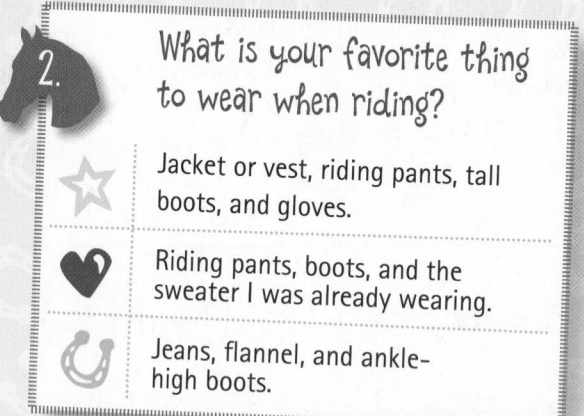

2. What is your favorite thing to wear when riding?

☆ Jacket or vest, riding pants, tall boots, and gloves.

❤ Riding pants, boots, and the sweater I was already wearing.

🐎 Jeans, flannel, and ankle-high boots.

3. Who do you admire the most?

🐎 "Horse whisperers."

☆ Dressage and jumper riders.

❤ My best friend.

4. What do you want to be when you grow up?

❤ I don't know yet.

☆ Stable owner.

🐎 Professional horse trainer.

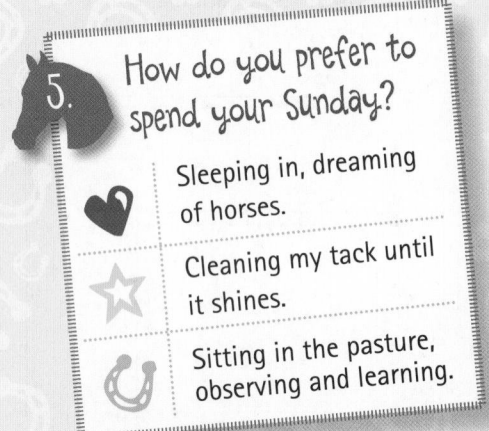

5. How do you prefer to spend your Sunday?

❤ Sleeping in, dreaming of horses.

☆ Cleaning my tack until it shines.

🐎 Sitting in the pasture, observing and learning.

CREATE A GUIDE LIKE THIS AND MARK OFF YOUR ANSWERS:

☆ 1 2 3 4 5 6 7 8 9 10

❤ 1 2 3 4 5 6 7 8 9 10

🐎 1 2 3 4 5 6 7 8 9 10

6. What is your goal in one year?

- ☆ Competing at a big-time show.
- ♥ Riding, riding, riding.
- ♘ On a horseback camping trip.

7. Which picture would you hang up on your wall?

8. Where would you like to go on a riding vacation?

- ♘ A ranch where you have to catch the horse you will ride from a herd, ride out all day, and sleep by a campfire.
- ☆ A show barn that has a competition at the end of the trip.
- ♥ By the ocean, near the mountains, on the moon...as long as there's horses!

9. Where is your favorite place to ride?

- ♘ The show grounds.
- ☆ In the arena.
- ♥ Who cares, as long as I'm with horses?

10. What does your dream horse look like?

- ♥ Just like my favorite pony at my riding school.
- ☆ Like a fancy show horse with a braided mane.
- ♘ A Paint or Appaloosa with lots of color!

Which answer did you pick most:

 ☆, ♘ or ♥ ? Here, you can see what it means.

☆ COMPETITIVE RIDER

The type of riding that most learn to compete at the highest levels someday is English. This kind of saddle can be seen in dressage, jumping, and eventing competitions. You sit up straight in the saddle, legs at an angle, and hold the reins with both hands. That way you're always in contact with the horse's mouth. Competitive riders often look pretty fancy: jackets, tall boots, white riding breeches, and gloves. If you love jumping or dressage, then the English riding style is the one for you.

♘ WESTERN RIDER

Western riding used to be crucial to how American cowboys did their jobs. There was a time when they had to drive herds of cattle for long distances over massive ranchlands. Today, Western riding and ranch work are sports. You've probably seen a Western saddle before, sometimes with fancy decorations and always with the horn at the front. That's where cowboys attach one end of their lasso when roping cattle. In a Western saddle, you lean back with your legs nearly straight down. For long rides it's quite comfortable! Western riders often steer their horses with only one hand, which requires a lot of experience. Much about the style is well-suited for long rides on varied terrain.

♥ JUST FOR FUN

You're open to everything and like to try new things, whether it's riding in the arena or out on the trail, dressage or jumping, vaulting or groundwork. You don't want to commit to just one riding style. Riding attire, saddle and bridle type—these aren't that important to you either. The main thing is that it all works. If it does, that's a-okay! After all, you love your horse, you love riding, and it's a ton of fun for you – no matter if on horseback or leading him, in the stall, or out in the pasture!

My First Riding Test

If I want to participate in horse shows, Susan expects me to have learned a lot about horses and riding! In some places, you get certified to ride horses on the trail, in dressage, or jumping...or for vaulting, driving, groundwork, reining, and working equitation.

How do I prepare myself?

Some riding schools offer clinics or camps with "tests" at the end. That way you can learn and practice specific skills in a group, and then be quizzed on it. (You'll find lots of knowledge in this book that will help you pass!)

Trotting over poles.

You need to practice saluting the judge! Some riding stables use side reins on ponies to ensure riders stay in control.

What Should Be Tested?

A riding test at your barn or at horseback riding camp checks what you know about horses and riding. It's all about showing what you know in practice. Depending on where you ride, it might include pointing out and naming the different parts of a horse's body, correctly putting on a bridle, cleaning tack, or performing groundwork exercises.

Who can point to the horse's fetlock?

Test Anxiety

Don't worry, occasional riding tests from your instructors should motivate you and be fun. The judges want you to succeed. If you have test anxiety, talk to your riding teacher about it. Since it's mostly about proving that you can ride, you really don't have to talk much!

How do you check the length of the stirrups??

Praise is important!

One round of canter.

Nail the Basics

The foundation of being a good horse person is horse knowledge. You can do this before learning to ride!

Learning Never Stops

Even if tested and told you are on your way to fulfilling your horse dream, remember that learning with horses never stops. Even the oldest, most experienced horse trainer should read new books and strive to always be acquiring new knowledge.

YOU PASS!

Being told you have the skills and knowledge to handle and ride your horse is such a great feeling!

Vaulting and Driving

If you love horses and like to do gymnastics, then vaulting is just the right sport for you. You are part of a team and learn to be super-flexible and balanced. Competitive driving is pretty elaborate because you need a horse, a carriage, and a harness. That's why people usually don't become drivers until they are adults.

Riding Camp

Hurray, I'm off to riding camp! An entire week without my brothers. I get to ride twice a day and hang out with my best riding friends. What could be better?

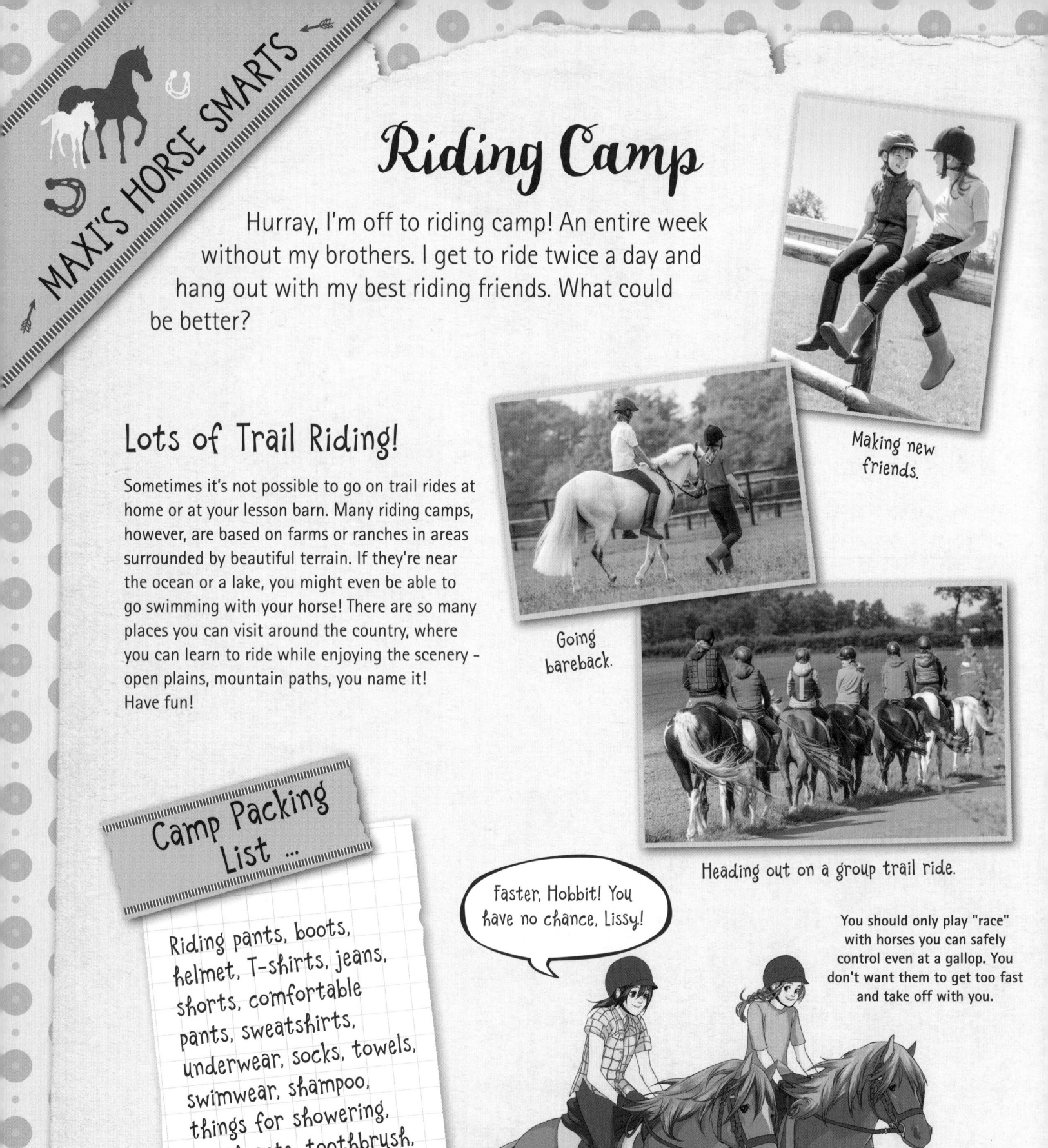

Making new friends.

Lots of Trail Riding!

Sometimes it's not possible to go on trail rides at home or at your lesson barn. Many riding camps, however, are based on farms or ranches in areas surrounded by beautiful terrain. If they're near the ocean or a lake, you might even be able to go swimming with your horse! There are so many places you can visit around the country, where you can learn to ride while enjoying the scenery – open plains, mountain paths, you name it! Have fun!

Going bareback.

Heading out on a group trail ride.

Camp Packing List ...

Riding pants, boots, helmet, T-shirts, jeans, shorts, comfortable pants, sweatshirts, underwear, socks, towels, swimwear, shampoo, things for showering, toothpaste, toothbrush, hairbrush, sunscreen, bug repellant, bedding, books, my journal

Faster, Hobbit! You have no chance, Lissy!

You should only play "race" with horses you can safely control even at a gallop. You don't want them to get too fast and take off with you.

What Type of Camp Suits Me?

I want to spend as much time as possible with horses. Mom and I looked around on the internet. There are so many horse camps that look amazing! I don't want one too far away, though, so my parents can drive me there. Ask around at your barn and check with your riding friends to see if they have a tip about where they enjoyed their trip.

I dreamed of sitting by a campfire and singing.

Homesickness

If you start missing your parents, call them. I did that on my second night away. I didn't drink enough water and got a headache, and I wished I could be with my mom. Lena brought me something to drink and cheered me up, which was really nice. Next morning everything was all right again.

RULES

Of course there are lots of rules at horse camp: set the table, clear the table, be on time, make your bed. And if all the boots pile up next to the door there will be chaos. When everyone does their part, there's no problem.

A daily task: catch your pony in the pasture while everyone else joins you.

With or Without Your Best Friend?

It's the most fun to plan to go to horse camp with your best friend. But if that doesn't work out, don't be afraid to be brave and go without someone. There are almost always others who are excited to make new friends.

Horse Power Party

For my birthday, I knew I wanted a horse-themed party. Same for you? Take a look at the next few pages to see all the things you can create for your "I Love Horses" Party: invitations, cake, prizes, and even your own horse!

For the invitations you'll need:

- Single-color cards
- Old horse magazines
- Scissors and glue stick
- Gel or paint pens

Like this example!

1. The Invitations

- Cut out pictures of horses from the magazines and glue them onto the cards
- Decorate them with the gel or paint pens
- You can pick the perfect picture for each friend that you invite. Create it just the way that friend will like best!

Or this one!

Or with a super-cute foal!

76

2. ♡ The Ribbon Garland

- Draw flower shapes onto the blue cardboard and cut them out.
- Cut a circle out of the gold and brown cardboard. One should be a little bit larger than the other. You can use a juice glass, a compass, or a glue stick as a template to trace.
- Cut out two long strips from the gold cardboard, and cut out a little triangle out of the bottom of each. Glue everything together.
- Tape your ribbons onto a long piece of string. It'll make a great garland for the party!

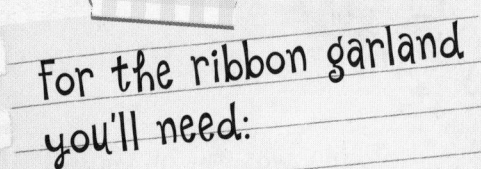

For the ribbon garland you'll need:

- Blue, brown, and gold cardboard
- Pencil and scissors
- Compass or something round as a template
- Crafting glue, tape
- String

3. ✿ Place Cards, Food, and Drinks

- Write the names of your guests on the ribbons with gold gel pen. Tape the ribbons onto straws. These are your place cards for your party table!

  - Guess what kind of drinks you should serve at an "I Love Horses" Party? Carrot or apple juice, of course! Believe it or not, they taste great when you mix them together!

    - Help your parents bake you a simple, flat, sheet cake. Color your frosting with green food coloring and spread it over the cake. Add sugar flowers and toy horse figurines to turn your cake into a pasture!

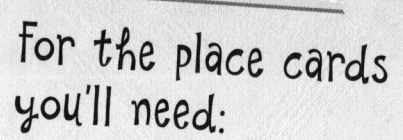

For the place cards you'll need:

- Homemade ribbons
- Gold gel pen
- Tape and straws

You can often find colorful straws at discount, party, or office supply stores.

Maxi's Tip

Are you going to have cookies or candy at your birthday? Take a look at the packaging: Some cookies and candy have gold foil inside the box or tin, perfect for your ribbons! You can also find metallic foil at arts-and-crafts stores.

My Birthday

From now on, Hobbit comes in packs of two

Today was my birthday! It was the best birthday I've ever had. After all, I've never turned twelve before. But that wasn't the only reason. The present I got from Mom and Dad was amazing: MY OWN PONY! No, not a live one, but one made out of wood. It's in our yard now, and I named it Hobbit. Now I can ride whenever I want. And I don't even have to muck out a stall! My brothers all put their allowances together and bought me a hoof pick. Leo gave me a broken toy car.

The second big surprise came in the afternoon. Mom, Dad, and the boys told me to get in the car and all together we drove to the barn. A garland was hanging over Hobbit's stall that said HAPPY BIRTHDAY. Susan and Lissy were there, and others from my riding lessons (even Elena), and there was a beautiful birthday cake.

"What...? Why...? Huh...?" I stuttered.

"Happy birthday, Maxi!" cried Susan, hugging me. "Your parents organized all of this," she whispered to me. My parents? Really? I couldn't believe it. Susan handed me a gift – a book about horses. Elena congratulated me and said she'd do my muck chores for me one day the coming week. Cool! Everyone sang "Happy Birthday" to me. Then I got to blow out the twelve candles on the cake. What did I wish for? Isn't it obvious...

Next, Lissy came up to me, saying, "Happy birthday," as she handed me a small package. I opened it really carefully because the wrapping paper with horses on it was so pretty. Inside there was a necklace with horse charms! Lissy blushed a bit. "I made it myself," she said.

"It's so pretty!" I replied and put it on right away. Hobbit nickered.

"He wants to congratulate you, too," said Susan, so I gave him a scratch right under his mane where he likes it.

"Cake?" Dad asked from behind me.

Everyone got a piece of cake, and Hobbit got one of my homemade horse cookies. At some point Lissy and the other kids from my lesson group had to go home. Elena had to go pick out a pasture. My brothers were playing soccer out in the parking lot.

"I still have a little bit of time before the next riding lesson," said Susan. "Would you like to ride Hobbit? As a birthday present, and so you can show your parents what you have learned."

Of course I wanted to! I brushed and saddled Hobbit while explaining to Mom and Dad what I was doing every step of the way. Then we went into the arena, and I rode a few rounds: at a walk, a trot, and even a canter. Hobbit did everything so well! I slowed him down and rode over to Mom and Dad where they stood near the doorway.

You should have seen how they looked!

"Wow!" Mom said.

And Dad said, "Wow-eee-wow!"

"What was that?" Susan asked with a laugh.

"We are thoroughly impressed," Dad explained, "with everything Maxi can do! She seems to be a really talented horseback rider."

"Indeed, she is," said Susan, and I smiled from ear to ear.

"Hobbit taught me everything I know," I said.

Susan coughed, and Mom and Dad laughed. I don't even know why. I just cuddled up to Hobbit and hugged him really tight.

Your Own Hobby Horse Show!

An "I Love Horses" Party is serious fun! The highlight was our Hobby Horse Show. We all crafted our own hobby horses at the party - we practically flew over all the obstacles!

For the hobby horse you'll need:

- Old socks (one sock that's intact and a few others with holes - old T-shirts work, too!)
- Scisssors and crafting glue
- Dowel or stick (around 3 feet long)
- String
- Pieces of felt for the mane (8 to 12 inches long)
- 2 googley eyes
- 2 adhesive furniture gliders or felt circles
- Felt scraps for the ears
- Ribbon for the halter and reins (3 feet)
- Clothes pins

1. The Hobby Horse

- Cut the old fabric into strips. Stuff the foot of the intact sock full of the other scraps. Stick one end of the pole into the sock, then keep stuffing until the sock is almost full. Tie a piece of string tight around the bottom of the sock. Cut the ends off short.

- Fold the felt for the mane in half and cut it almost to the crease. Glue it on the stuffed sock as the mane. Glue on the googley eyes and then the furniture gliders or felt circles – those are going to be the nostrils.

- For the ears, cut two triangles out of the remaining felt. Cut a slit about three-quarters of an inch into the bottom and place the two halves one over the other. Glue the ears onto the head.

- Cut three pieces of ribbon for the halter: one each for the noseband, the headstall and throatlatch, and the cheek pieces.

- Glue the overlapping parts together and hold them together with clothespins until they dry. Tie on the reins on the left and right side.

We even named our hobby horses! The name of mine was Hobbit, of course. Lissy's "pony," Tapir, refused one of the jumps we set up, and she fell down. We made it just like when you're riding in real life! It was so fun. My birthday party couldn't have been any better.

2. ♥ THE SHOW

- Set up a jump course made of boxes or stacks of books and broomsticks. A slalom or barrel course made of soda bottles or a seesaw (made of a long wooden board resting on a block of wood in the middle) are fun obstacles for trail course in your show. Think of other ideas!
- Draw a big "1" onto one of the ribbons you made for your garland. Tape a clothespin to the back of the ribbon.

Use the clothespin to attach the ribbon to the bridle of the winning horse.

If it's nice out you can have your hobby horse show outdoors. You can go on a treasure hunt trail ride in the woods or line up all together and race on the playground with hobby horses!

Maxi's Tip

Make little goody bags for all your friends who come to your party. You can tape ribbons onto those, too, and write everyone's names on them! Put treats for (real) horses, as well as your guests, inside.

A Horse of Your Own

I constantly imagine what it would be like to have my own horse. I would ride every day. My horse would whinny whenever I arrive. I would love it more than anything else in the world. "When you earn your own money," my parents say, "you can have a pony." So I guess I still have to wait before my dream will come true.

A pony is a friend for life!

Buying a Horse

It's not so easy to find the right horse or pony for yourself. You really have to think about what you want to do with your future horse: dressage, jumping, or Western riding; horse shows or going on trail rides - lots of possibilities!

A beginning or novice rider should definitely buy an "educated," well-trained horse because it takes a ton of experience to teach a horse properly. Young horses really need a patient and capable person at their side, otherwise a lot of things could go wrong.

Maybe your dream horse is your favorite horse at your lesson barn, just like Hobbit is mine? You also have to think about the fact that you're still going to grow - size can be an issue. Will you be too big and heavy for a medium-sized pony next year? As you can see, there are many things to take into consideration. It is important to have help from a knowledgeable horse person. By the way, if your parents and you decide to really do it, there is paperwork involved they will probably have to handle. Your horse may have registration papers and insurance, plus purchase and sales or lease agreements, which have to be signed by someone 18 or over.

If I got to pick the perfect horse for me, it would be Hobbit!

When your horse trusts you, he'll be happy to come with you, wherever you are going.

MONTHLY COSTS

What does a horse need?

→ Stall or shed with access to pasture

→ Hay, grain (sometimes), and water

→ Vaccinations, dewormer, and medication from a veterinarian

→ Regular hoof care from a farrier

Depending on where you live and whether you board your new horse or have him at home, this can be hundreds or thousands of dollars.

Owning and caring for your own pony is truly wonderful!

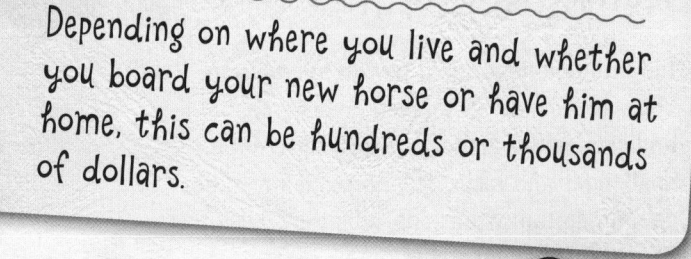

Maxi's Tip

Ride as many different horses as possible. That way you will get to know many different horses' characters and reactions and will be able to handle them appropriately. This will help you later on with your own horse.

Leasing a Horse

When you lease a horse, you help care for him but someone else owns him. It is almost like having your own horse. Maybe you could convince your parents to let you do this? It's not as expensive, the responsibility for the animal lies mainly with the owner, and this way you can figure out if you can really make the time in your life and love a horse like you dream of doing.

Games on Horseback

My friend Lissy and I are at the barn. The mounted games are taking place today. We're a team with one horse (Hobbit!) and are already super excited. We take turns riding while the other leads. We can't wait to see which games we get to play!

Agility and Fun

Mounted games should be fun for everyone. You will learn to sit relaxed on a horse and keep your balance through different challenges and tasks. The horses learn to be calm in certain situations, plus they get lots of attention – and treats!

IDEAS FOR GAMES

- Weaving through a slalom course
- Sticking whips in a line of cones
- Balancing cups of water
- Drawing pictures while trotting
- Balancing an egg on a spoon
- Treasure hunt
- Navigating through poles
- Barrel race

Slalom with Neck Ring

Can you weave your pony through a slalom course using only a neck ring? Touch the ring to the right side of the neck and the horse will turn left.

Umbrella and Cavalletti

Can you ride with one hand? For this game, make sure your pony is not scared of umbrellas.

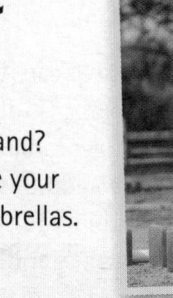

Go Ahead and Dress Up!

Mounted games are even more fun when your horse is decorated and you are all dressed up. Sometimes you can even earn some extra points with cool costumes. The most important thing is that you are wearing closed-toe shoes and a helmet when you are on horseback.

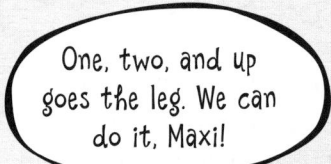

MORE GAMES

• Sing a song while gargling
• Play charades
• Three-legged race
• Costume contest
• Horsey pictionary

Helmets look great with decoration, such as a pair of ears or a veil.

One, two, and up goes the leg. We can do it, Maxi!

1. Some mounted games are only for advanced riders as everything is done at a canter. In this one, you remove the cup and place it on the next pole!

2. For the game "Blindfolded Leader," the rider is not allowed to steer but has to tell her blindfolded partner how to lead the way.

Off to the Show!

Today I'm off to my first horse show. I am going with Susan, which is exciting! She signed up for a jumping and dressage show at another farm nearby.

Braiding

To get a horse's mane braids to be as even as possible takes a lot of practice. What a good thing that Hobbit just stands there so patiently.

What Kind of Show?

There are many different kinds and levels of riding competitions in North America. In some areas, there are local shows with classes for both English and Western riders. If you ride a certain breed of horse, you might go to shows put on by a breed organization, like the AQHA (American Quarter Horse Association). Some people prefer to jump and will look for hunter-jumper competitions. Others like dressage and may go to shows affiliated with the USDF (United States Dressage Federation).

Spotless white breeches, clean gloves, and shiny boots are part of proper show wear for English riders.

WHAT CLASSES SHOULD I ENTER?

Depending on the kind of show you go to, there may be different levels to enter. This may be determined by your riding ability or your horse's experience. A grownup who knows you and your horse well should help you choose your classes.

The most important thing is not to enter too many classes with your horse, whatever your discipline. He should enjoy the show experience, too, and he shouldn't be overworked and exhausted.

Show Style

Riders may also want to braid their own hair for shows. It looks neater and the judges can evaluate your posture more easily.

Your hair should be neatly styled for a horse show. French braids look great and they fit under your helmet.

I think I'm in the wrong trailer!

SHOW HORSE

Start Small and Fun

When first trying competitions, it can help to begin with a small show and just participate to have fun with your horse and your friends. There are many ways you can be part of smaller shows without having to enter classes that might make you nervous: some offer costume contests, pleasure mount classes, and trail classes. It is also lots of fun to just go and watch a horse show, by the way. Why don't you ask at your barn? Maybe somebody knows where and when the next show is taking place.

Transportation

Trailering horses from place to place is nothing to be taken for granted. All horses need to be trained to safely load and unload, as well as being tied in a moving vehicle over both short and long distances. Some horses are afraid of stepping inside horse trailers. You have to carefully and patiently work with them through this challenge – ideally with the help of an expert.

Horsemanship Test

If you are in Pony Club or 4-H, you may have horse knowledge tests. These are not about riding, driving, or vaulting, but rather about your knowledge and proficiency in all things horse. Even if you aren't in a club, you can ask your instructor to quiz you or give yourself tests at home.

10 BASIC HORSE KNOWLEDGE QUESTIONS – TRY IT!

1. How should you approach a horse?

a Run to the paddock, calling his name at the gate.

b Sneak up on him from behind so he doesn't see me right away.

c Approach from the front or the side and say his name in a friendly voice.

2. What is the most important safety tip when tying a horse?

a He has to be tied up in such a way that he can't get loose.

b He should be tied with a very short rope.

c You should use a safety knot.

3. How do I earn the horse's trust?

a I give him all the nicest tack and equipment.

b I am understanding and patient in stressful situations.

c I feed him lots of treats.

4. What is a paddock?

a A small, enclosed area with sand or grass footing.

b A big stall with a window that opens to the outside.

c A thick saddle pad.

(Solutions: 1c, 2c, 3b, 4a, 5a, 6a, 7b, 8c, 9b, 10a)

5.

What is TPR?

a The horse's temperature, pulse, and respiration.

b The temperature in the barn.

c The results at a three-day event.

6.

What should you do if your horse ate a poisonous plant?

a Call a vet right away and save some pieces of the plant, if possible.

b Let the horse drink lots of water.

c Wait and see what happens.

7.

What is a gray?

a An older horse with white spots.

b A horse with a white coat, mane, and tail.

c A horse with a white mane.

8.

Where on a horse are the chestnuts?

a In the feed tub.

b At the dock of the tail.

c On the legs.

9.

How tall is a horse?

a Over 14 hands at the withers.

b Over 14.2 hands at the withers.

c Under 18 hands at the withers.

10.

What is roughage?

a Hay and straw.

b Pelleted feed.

c Carrots.

DRESSAGE FACTS

➡ Dressage was developed by the Greek military, with the earliest known writing dating to 400 BC.

➡ It became an Olympic sport in 1912.

➡ Horses and riders perform prescribed movements in the form of a "test."

➡ Movements are scored 0-10, with 0 meaning you didn't do it, and 10 being excellent.

JUMPING FACTS

➡ Jumping classes first became popular in Europe around 1900.

➡ An Italian riding instructor, Captain Federico Caprilli, is credited for developing what is known as the "forward seat," which we use over fences.

TRAIL RIDING FACTS

➡ There are ways to compete, even if your favorite thing to do is trail ride! There are competitive trail rides and distance rides around the country and the world.

➡ Some of the best riding vacations involve trail riding! You can ride out West, on an African safari, and on treks in South America! Pretty cool.

Can a horse have a fever?

(He has a fever at 102.2 degrees Fahrenheit - call the vet!)

Horse Camping

Adventures and Campfires

It's already been one year since I started riding. Hobbit and I are best friends, just like Lissy and I. Of course she and I were beyond excited when Susan announced a riding campout! "Two days in the saddle, and in between that, one night in the hay." Could there be anything more beautiful?

A few weeks later we were off. Lissy's dad loaded the sleeping bags and backpacks with our clothes into his car. He drove all of our stuff to a farm we were going to ride to and then spend the night in the barn. Even though he drove the big stuff, my saddle bags were full to the brim: food, drinks, a rain jacket, and Mom's cell phone. "Just in case..." she said. Susan had a map with her, too, of course, as well as a first aid kit for horses and humans, mosquito repellent, and a bunch of other practical things.

"It's time to go," I whispered to Hobbit when we rode away from the stable. I caressed his neck and loosened the reins. We both knew the first stretch of the ride by heart so we could relax a little. After a while, though, we turned onto a path I had never ridden along before. I shortened the reins and gathered Hobbit a little bit. Now there was no more time for daydreaming, I had to pay attention! In the forest, the path leisurely led uphill. Around noon we had reached the peak and stopped for a break at a spring.

"Ouch, my butt!" said Lissy when we got back on. She groaned and looked very tortured.

"Mine too," I whispered. "But we're going to persevere, okay?"

Two more hours to go! Our moods slowly worsened. Our bottoms and legs were burning as if they were on fire. Horseflies were swarming around us and

the horses. I already had three bites that itched like crazy despite the cream Susan gave me.

"I wish we were there already," grumbled Lissy. Out of pure frustration she whacked a bush that was growing right next to the path with her crop.

That did it. Tapir, who was nearly dozing off before, jolted up. I saw the white in his eyes light up as he spooked and took off. Lissy clung on desperately. Hobbit was startled as well and wanted to follow, but he couldn't get around Lauri, Susan's huge Friesian.

Susan wasted no time. "Everyone, dismount! Elena, keep watch," she directed. Then she gave Lauri the aids to canter and rode off after Lissy and Tapir.

We dismounted. "It's okay, buddy. Everything's okay," I murmured to Hobbit. That calmed him down, and me, too. My God, what a shock! Hobbit almost took off with me! But what about Lissy and Tapir? Were they okay?

Finally the two horses came back into view. I gave Elena Hobbit's reins and ran to meet Lissy and Tapir. She gave me a smile with red cheeks.

"Sorry, guys!" she called to the group. "That was really dumb of me."

Susan nodded. "It sure was. It was your own fault that Tapir spooked. Luckily nothing more happened and you are both okay." She handed everyone a little piece of candy - horses and humans. The sweet sugar gave me another burst of energy, and I was able to enjoy the last stretch of the long ride.

The farm where we were going to spend the night had a river running through it. We all went for a dip, riders and ponies, and it was lovely. At the campfire we got to have hotdogs and s'mores. It wasn't until very late that we crawled into our sleeping bags, which were spread out on top of the hay in the barn loft. We could hear the horses downstairs in their stalls, scraping their hooves, chewing, and nickering.

"Goodnight, Maxi," said Lissy next to me.

"Goodnight, Lissy." In my dream I was still riding Hobbit, the very best pony in the whole wide world.